THE
NEWLYWED
COOKBOOK

THE NEWLYWED COOKBOOK

COOKING HAPPILY EVER AFTER

ROXANNE WYSS
&
KATHY MOORE

Photographs by
DAVID SHAUGHNESSY

ST. MARTIN'S GRIFFIN
NEW YORK

Printed in China.

For information, address St. Martin's Press,
175 Fifth Avenue, New York, N.Y. 10010.

www.stmartins.com

Book design by Rita Sowins / Sowins Design
Lifestyle photographs by Shutterstock
Production Manager: Lisa Viviani Goris

The Library of Congress Cataloging-in-Publication
Data is available upon request.

ISBN 978-1-250-05436-4 (paper over board)
ISBN 978-1-4668-6844-1 (e-book)

St. Martin's Griffin books may be purchased for
educational, business, or promotional use. For
information on bulk purchases, please contact
Macmillan Corporate and Premium Sales Department at 1-800-221-7945, extension 5442, or write
specialmarkets@macmillan.com.

First Edition: January 2015

10 9 8 7 6 5 4 3 2 1

The book is dedicated to each of our parents.
Roxanne's parents, Kenny and Colleen Wyss, and Kathy's parents,
Ben and Ella Mae Ervin, blessed us by modeling the best of marriage.
Their commitment and love for each other inspire us
and allow us to rejoice with all newlyweds at
the prospects of their bright and loving futures.

CONTENTS

INTRODUCTION

No time in life is as exciting and new, and yes, sometimes as challenging as your first year of marriage. While the wedding bells may have stopped ringing, your hearts are beating loudly with love and romance as you start this journey together.

It is a time of sharing new experiences, building memories that will last a lifetime, and establishing sacred traditions. It is a year of leisurely weekends built around busy evenings that are so much sweeter since you share them with the love of your life. It is a year of many firsts—first holidays, first dinner parties, first visits from your in-laws, and even your first anniversary.

It is also a time for building routines and carving out habits that will define your life as a couple. The kitchen is no longer the wife's domain. Instead, it is a shared sanctuary, where you start your day and where you seek refuge after a busy day. It is where you will grow and learn, and soon you will discover together why the kitchen is the heart of the home.

Rules no longer apply—and that is what makes it so fun. The kitchen, your cooking style, and the menu plans are yours for you to create together. Discover if casual or elegant, traditional or adventuresome, mild or spicy, or some fun combination of

all of these is your style. Blend your tastes and approaches together so they define you as a couple and lead you to a happy, healthy lifestyle.

Your gifts and the wedding registry you created are a reflection of the two of you. Gone are the days of registering for fine china, sterling silver candlesticks, and chafing dishes; no longer do couples register just for classic (while sometimes useless) pieces or for what the bride or her mom thought should be included. Today's couples together select functional and colorful dishes and appliances that are an expression of their lifestyle. Colorful, casual dinnerware; wine, beer, or cocktail glasses;

heavy-duty stand mixers, food processors, espresso makers, waffle makers, and ice cream makers; top-quality cutlery; professional-quality blenders; and deluxe slow cookers are just a few of the items that today's couples want. All of those dishes, utensils, and equipment will make the cooking easier and more fun. The food you create will taste better and be more attractive to serve for years to come.

Turn to the back of this cookbook for helpful kitchen tips that will make cooking easier and an indispensable guide to organizing the kitchen, grocery shopping, and stocking the pantry. You will also learn how to select and use the pots, pans, bakeware, utensils, and appliances that will make your kitchen a dream come true.

Now, it is time to cook together and build a lifetime of love and good eating.

APPLIANCE
PRO

Shiny new appliances are thrilling, and with the touch of a button you can whip, simmer, sizzle, slice, blend, bake, or brew and more easily cook like a pro. They make the cooking tasks tastier, easier, and faster! But how? This chapter has recipes to get you started, but for more tips on selecting and using those new appliances, turn to Small Appliance 101 (page 177).

APPLIANCE TIPS:

» Read the booklet or information packed with the appliance, or visit the manufacturer's website for tips on using the appliance and safety recommendations. Write the date you received the appliance on the outside of the use and care information and keep it. (We bet for many appliances, it will be your wedding date, and what a fun reminder of that special day.) You want to note the date if future questions arise regarding service, accessory parts, or the warranty. Slip the information leaflets into plastic sleeves and keep them all in a three-ring notebook, or scan the information and make an electronic file for easy reference. Be sure to complete the warranty or registration card and submit it or mail it to the manufacturer in case of malfunction, questions, or possible recalls.

CREAMY TOMATO SOUP
with PEPE PASTA

You don't need to feel under the weather to enjoy this soup. The ingredients come together quickly, and this is the perfect antidote for a stressful day. At Roxanne's house, this is always served with a crusty grilled cheese sandwich.

3 TABLESPOONS OLIVE OIL

2 MEDIUM YELLOW ONIONS, CHOPPED

4 CLOVES GARLIC, MINCED

1 (32-OUNCE) CARTON REDUCED-SODIUM CHICKEN BROTH

1 (28-OUNCE) CAN CRUSHED TOMATOES

1 TEASPOON DRIED BASIL LEAVES

1 TEASPOON GRANULATED SUGAR

2 TEASPOONS KOSHER SALT

1 TEASPOON COARSELY GROUND BLACK PEPPER

¼ CUP ACINI DI PEPE PASTA

½ CUP HEAVY CREAM

SERVES 6

Heat the olive oil in a 6-quart Dutch oven over medium-high heat. Add the onions and reduce the heat to medium-low; continue to cook, stirring frequently, for 15 minutes, until the onions are golden brown. Add the garlic and cook for 30 seconds.

Add the chicken broth, tomatoes, basil leaves, sugar, salt, and pepper. Bring the soup to a boil and then reduce the heat to maintain a simmer. Simmer for 15 minutes. Remove the pot from the stove. Using an immersion blender, puree the soup until smooth. Return the soup to the stove and bring to a boil. Add the pasta and cook for 7 to 8 minutes more, until pasta is cooked.

Stir in the cream. Cook, stirring frequently, just until the soup returns to a simmer. Serve warm.

TIPS:

» This soup can be made a day or two ahead and reheated.

» What is pepe pasta? Italians refer to this pasta as acini di pepe. It is a small, round pasta traditionally used in soups. The name translates to peppercorns. If you are unable to locate pepe pasta in your grocery store, you can substitute orzo pasta.

» If you don't have an immersion blender, use your countertop blender. Carefully ladle the soup into the blender in batches so as not to overfill the container and take care not to exceed the "max fill" line. Vent the blender lid to allow heat and steam to escape. Begin at low speed.

MOJITO SLUSHIE

Pour a cool and refreshing Mojito Slushie on a hot summer day. This recipe makes just enough for two servings—so the two of you can plan a leisurely afternoon by the pool or in the hammock. When friends gather, make a double batch or more, and let the party begin!

½ CUP GRANULATED SUGAR

¼ CUP FRESH MINT LEAVES, PLUS
    4 TO 6 MINT LEAVES

¼ CUP LIGHT RUM

¼ CUP FRESH LIME JUICE

2 CUPS ICE CUBES

MINT LEAVES AND LIME SLICES OR
    THIN WEDGES, FOR GARNISH

SERVES 2

Heat together the sugar, ¼ cup of the mint leaves, and ½ cup water in a 1-quart saucepan over medium heat. Use the back of a spoon to bruise (and muddle) the mint leaves. Cook, stirring frequently, until the sugar syrup comes to a boil and the sugar dissolves.

Remove the pan from the heat and allow it to stand at room temperature for 1 hour or up to 8 hours, so mint infuses the sugar syrup.

Strain the sugar syrup through a fine-mesh strainer into a blender. Discard the mint leaves in the strainer. Add the rum, lime juice, remaining 4 to 6 fresh mint leaves, and ice cubes. Blend until the mixture is smooth and slushy and the ice is finely chopped. Pour the slushies into glasses and garnish each with fresh mint leaves and a lime slice or wedge.

TIPS:

» For make-ahead convenience, make the mint sugar syrup early in the day or the day before. Strain the syrup into a refrigerator container, then cover and refrigerate the syrup until ready to use.

» Serving a crowd? You will want to have plenty ready to make quickly. Double or triple the mint syrup so you can make two drinks at a time. For two drinks, pour ½ cup of the syrup into the blender, add the remaining ingredients as directed, blend, and serve. Pour another ½ cup of the syrup into the blender, add the remaining ingredients, and let the party keep going.

» The volume of liquid and ice that a blender can handle varies by brand and model. Most blenders can easily handle blending two servings at a time and you can still serve a crowd.

CLASSIC BASIL PESTO

Making your own basil pesto is so quick and easy you will never have to purchase jars or containers of pesto at the store again. Toss the freshly made pesto on pasta, spoon it on top of grilled meat or chicken, spread it on a sandwich, or drizzle it over your soup to add a flavor punch. If one batch makes more than you need, freeze it for use at a later date.

2 CUPS FRESH BASIL LEAVES

¼ CUP PINE NUTS, TOASTED

1 TO 2 CLOVES GARLIC, HALVED

½ TEASPOON KOSHER SALT

¼ TEASPOON COARSELY GROUND
    BLACK PEPPER

⅔ CUP EXTRA-VIRGIN OLIVE OIL

½ CUP FRESHLY GRATED
    PARMESAN CHEESE

MAKES ABOUT 1 CUP

Combine the basil, pine nuts, garlic, salt, and pepper in the work bowl of a food processor. Pulse to finely chop. While the food processor is running, add the oil in a steady stream and continue processing until smooth.

Place the pesto in a bowl and stir in the Parmesan.

TIPS:

» Substitute chopped walnuts for the pine nuts, if desired.

» Toasting the pine nuts or walnuts intensifies the flavor. To toast the nuts, spread them in a single layer on a baking sheet. Toast in a pre-heated 350°F oven for 5 to 7 minutes, or until lightly toasted.

» Store prepared pesto, covered, in the refrigerator for up to 3 days, or cover it, label, and freeze for longer storage. To use, thaw overnight in the refrigerator.

» Freshly grated Parmesan cheese adds more flavor than packaged shredded Parmesan cheese. To grate the Parmesan cheese, use a rasp-style grater, such as a Microplane. To "grate" this hard cheese in a food processor, allow the Parmesan to come to room temperature, cut it into 1-inch cubes, and place them in the work bowl of the food processor fitted with the metal chopping blade; pulse to very finely chop.

SUN-DRIED TOMATO PESTO

Once you experience the flavor of this pesto, you will think of a plethora of ways to use this Italian staple. Tossed with hot cooked pasta, spooned over goat cheese, spread on paninis, or used as a pizza sauce, it's perfection!

1 (8.5-OUNCE) JAR SUN-DRIED
    TOMATOES PACKED IN OLIVE OIL
    WITH ITALIAN HERBS

2 TABLESPOONS EXTRA-VIRGIN
    OLIVE OIL

¼ CUP TOMATO SAUCE

2 CLOVES GARLIC, HALVED

½ CUP FRESH BASIL LEAVES

½ CUP FRESH FLAT-LEAF PARSLEY

1 TEASPOON BALSAMIC VINEGAR

½ TEASPOON KOSHER SALT

¼ TEASPOON COARSELY GROUND
    BLACK PEPPER

½ CUP FRESHLY GRATED
    PARMESAN CHEESE

MAKES 1½ CUPS

Combine all the ingredients (including the oil in which the tomatoes are packed) in the work bowl of a food processor. Pulse to finely chop.

TIPS:

» Store prepared pesto, covered, in the refrigerator for up to 3 days, or cover it, label, and freeze for longer storage. To use, thaw overnight in the refrigerator.

» For a more intense basil flavor, prepare the recipe with all basil and omit the flat-leaf parsley.

» Freshly grated Parmesan cheese adds more flavor than packaged shredded Parmesan cheese. To grate the Parmesan cheese, use a rasp-style grater, such as a Microplane. To "grate" this hard cheese in a food processor, allow the Parmesan to come to room temperature, cut it into 1-inch cubes, and place them in the work bowl of the food processor fitted with the metal chopping blade; pulse to very finely chop.

ARUGULA PESTO

Arugula has a peppery mustard flavor that melds well into a pesto. If the arugula is hard to find, or if you enjoy a milder flavor, substitute fresh spinach.

4 CUPS ARUGULA

3 CLOVES GARLIC, HALVED

¼ CUP TOASTED WALNUTS

½ TEASPOON KOSHER SALT

¼ TEASPOON COARSELY GROUND
   BLACK PEPPER

⅔ CUP EXTRA-VIRGIN OLIVE OIL

1 CUP FRESHLY GRATED PARMESAN
   CHEESE

MAKES ABOUT 1 CUP

Combine the arugula, garlic, walnuts, salt, and pepper in the work bowl of a food processor. Pulse to finely chop. While the food processor is running, add the oil in a steady stream and continue processing until smooth.

Place the pesto in a bowl and stir in the Parmesan.

TIPS:

» Store prepared pesto, covered, in the refrigerator for up to 3 days, or cover it, label, and freeze for longer storage. To use, thaw overnight in the refrigerator.

» Freshly grated Parmesan cheese adds more flavor than packaged shredded Parmesan cheese. To grate the Parmesan cheese, use a rasp-style grater, such as a Microplane. To "grate" this hard cheese in a food processor, allow the Parmesan to come to room temperature, cut it into 1-inch cubes, and place them in the work bowl of the food processor fitted with the metal chopping blade; pulse to very finely chop.

» Toasting the walnuts intensifies the flavor. To toast the walnuts, spread them in a single layer on a baking sheet. Toast in a preheated 350°F oven for 5 to 7 minutes, or until lightly toasted.

CIDERHOUSE DUTCH APPLE PIE

Boiling the apple cider reduces it and creates a sweet syrup that is packed with an intense apple flavor. What this syrup adds to this apple pie is wonderful.

CRUST:

1½ CUPS ALL-PURPOSE FLOUR

½ TEASPOON TABLE SALT

½ CUP VEGETABLE SHORTENING

3 TO 4 TABLESPOONS ICE WATER

FILLING:

1 CUP APPLE CIDER

⅓ CUP GRANULATED SUGAR

⅓ CUP PACKED BROWN SUGAR

¼ CUP CORNSTARCH

½ TEASPOON GROUND
  CINNAMON

DASH OF TABLE SALT

9 MEDIUM GRANNY SMITH
  APPLES, PEELED, CORED, AND
  QUARTERED

1 TABLESPOON FRESH LEMON
  JUICE

MAKES 1 (9½-INCH) PIE

MAKE THE CRUST: Place the flour and salt in the work bowl of a food processor and pulse to combine. Add the vegetable shortening and process until the shortening is evenly cut into the flour and the mixture resembles coarse crumbs. Sprinkle evenly with 3 tablespoons of the ice water and continue to pulse just until the mixture comes together into a ball. Do not overwork. If the dough is still dry, add additional ice water, 1 teaspoon at a time, until the dough holds together. Gather the dough into a ball and flatten into a disc. Wrap the dough in plastic wrap and refrigerate it for several hours or overnight.

REDUCE THE CIDER: Bring the apple cider to a boil, uncovered, in a 6-quart saucepan or Dutch oven over medium-high heat. Reduce the heat to maintain a boil and cook, stirring frequently, for 7 to 8 minutes, or until the cider has reduced to ¼ cup. Watch the cider closely so it does not boil dry. When properly reduced, it will have a golden, amber color and be thick like syrup. Set the pan with cider off the heat and allow it to cool.

Preheat the oven to 425°F.

Place the prepared crust on a lightly floured work surface and roll it into a 12- to 13-inch circle. Carefully transfer the crust to a 9½ x 2-inch deep-dish pie pan. Trim the edges and crimp. Set aside.

If the following steps are done in order, there is no need to wash the work bowl in between the steps.

⅔ CUP ALL-PURPOSE FLOUR

¼ CUP GRANULATED SUGAR

¼ CUP PACKED BROWN SUGAR

5 TABLESPOONS COLD UNSALTED
   BUTTER, CUT INTO
   4 PIECES

MAKE THE STREUSEL: Place the flour, sugar, and brown sugar in the work bowl of a food processor and pulse to combine. Add the butter and pulse 10 to 12 times or until the butter is cut into small pieces and the mixture is crumbly; do not process until smooth. Remove the streusel from the work bowl and set aside.

MAKE THE FILLING: Place the sugar, brown sugar, cornstarch, cinnamon, and salt in the work bowl of a food processor and pulse to combine. Remove the filling from the work bowl and set aside.

Slice the apples thinly (about 4mm) using the slicing blade on the food processor. Pour the sliced apples into the cooled cider syrup in the pan. Add the lemon juice and toss to coat the apples evenly in syrup and lemon juice. Sprinkle the sugar-cornstarch mixture over the apples and toss to coat evenly. Heat, uncovered, over medium heat, stirring frequently, until the juices begin to boil. Cook, stirring frequently, for 3 minutes or just until the apples are hot and begin to soften. Spoon the hot apples into the prepared crust, scraping all sugary liquids onto the apples. Sprinkle the streusel evenly over the apples.

Place the pie on a rimmed baking sheet. Bake for 20 minutes. Reduce the oven temperature to 350°F. Carefully arrange strips of aluminum foil around the edges of the crust to prevent overbrowning. Bake for 35 to 40 minutes or until golden brown.

TIPS:

» You can make the entire pie without a food processor. For the crust and then for the streusel, mix the ingredients in a bowl; use a pastry cutter and cut the mixture until it forms even crumbs. For the filling, whisk together the sugar, brown sugar, cornstarch, cinnamon, and salt in a bowl until well blended. Slice the apples with a sharp knife. Proceed as directed above to cook and reduce the syrup, assemble the pie, and bake it.

GARDENER'S GRATIN

The extra time the Gardener's Gratin requires is time well spent, especially if you are married to a someone who isn't a vegetable lover. This recipe is perfect for using delicious gifts from the garden: tomatoes and zucchini, which always seem to be in abundance. Plan to prepare it on a day when you have a bit more time to spend in the kitchen. This would also be a memorable vegetarian entrée.

1 POUND MEDIUM ZUCCHINI, TRIMMED

1½ TEASPOONS KOSHER SALT

¾ POUND RIPE TOMATOES (ABOUT 2 LARGE), CUT INTO ¼-INCH SLICES

4 TABLESPOONS PLUS 2 TEASPOONS OLIVE OIL

1 MEDIUM ONION, HALVED AND THINLY SLICED

4 OUNCES BUTTON MUSHROOMS, THINLY SLICED

1 CLOVE GARLIC, MINCED

2 TEASPOONS FRESH THYME LEAVES, MINCED

1 SLICE SANDWICH BREAD

½ CUP SHREDDED PARMESAN CHEESE

SERVES 6 TO 8 AS A SIDE DISH OR 4 AS A MAIN COURSE

Preheat the oven to 400°F. Spray an 8 x 8 x 2-inch baking dish with nonstick spray.

Cut the zucchini into thin slices (about 4mm) using the slicing blade on the food processor. Place the slices in a colander and toss with 1 teaspoon of the salt. Place the colander over a bowl and allow it to stand for 40 minutes. Arrange the zucchini slices on layers of paper towels and cover with additional paper towels. Press to remove as much liquid as possible.

Place the tomato slices on a double layer of paper towels. Sprinkle the slices evenly with the remaining ½ teaspoon salt. Allow them to stand for 30 minutes. Top with additional paper towels and pat to remove as much liquid as possible.

Meanwhile, heat 1 tablespoon of the olive oil in a 12-inch nonstick skillet over medium heat. Add the onion slices and cook, stirring occasionally, for 10 to 15 minutes. Add the mushrooms and continue to cook for 5 to 10 minutes more, or until the moisture has evaporated from the mushrooms; set aside.

Stir together 3 tablespoons of the olive oil, the garlic, and the thyme in a small bowl.

Place the zucchini in a single layer in the prepared pan. Drizzle them with half of the olive oil–thyme mixture. Top with the caramelized onions and mushrooms, and then layer the tomato slices over the mushroom mixture. Drizzle with the remaining olive oil–thyme mixture.

Bake, uncovered, for 30 to 35 minutes or until the vegetables are just beginning to brown around the edges. Remove from the oven and increase the oven temperature to 425°F.

Process the bread in the food processor to make fresh bread crumbs; you will need ½ cup. Combine the fresh bread crumbs and Parmesan in a small bowl. Drizzle the remaining 2 teaspoons olive oil over the mixture and stir to combine. Sprinkle the crumbs evenly over the tomatoes.

Bake, uncovered, for 5 to 10 minutes, or until the cheese is melted and the bread crumbs are light brown. Allow to cool for at least 10 minutes before serving.

TIPS:

» Sprinkle with chopped fresh parsley or basil before serving.

CHICKEN CAPRESE PANINI

Traditionally, a caprese salad is a salad made with mozzarella, tomatoes, and basil and then drizzled with balsamic vinegar. Turn this salad into a quick dinner perfect for any day of the week.

2 SMALL BONELESS SKINLESS
   CHICKEN BREASTS, ABOUT 6
   OUNCES EACH
½ CUP PREPARED ZESTY ITALIAN
   DRESSING
KOSHER SALT AND FRESHLY
   GROUND BLACK PEPPER
CIABATTA BREAD OR FOCACCIA
   BREAD, HALVED HORIZONTALLY
   AND CUT INTO SANDWICH-SIZE
   SERVINGS
2 TOMATO SLICES
2 THICK SLICES FRESH
   MOZZARELLA CHEESE
6 TO 8 FRESH BASIL LEAVES
BALSAMIC VINEGAR

SERVES 2

Pound the chicken breasts between sheets of plastic wrap until the chicken is about ½ inch thick.

Place the chicken breasts in a zip-top bag (or in a shallow dish). Add the Italian dressing and seal the bag (or cover the dish), refrigerate, and marinate for 30 minutes or up to several hours.

Preheat a grill to medium-high or allow the coals to burn down to white ash.

Drain the chicken and discard the marinade. Season the chicken with salt and pepper. Grill the chicken for 5 to 6 minutes per side or until golden brown; the meat should no longer be pink inside and a meat thermometer inserted into the center of the meat should register 165°F. Place the chicken on a plate, cover with aluminum foil, and let it rest for 5 minutes.

Preheat a panini press. Place the chicken on the bottom slice of the bread. Top with tomato slices, mozzarella, and basil. Sprinkle balsamic vinegar on the cut side of the top bread slice and place it on the sandwich. Place the sandwich on the panini press, close, and toast for 2 to 3 minutes, or until the bread is toasted, the sandwich is hot, and the cheese has melted.

TIPS:

» The classic salad and this panini are made using fresh mozzarella, which is softer than typical factory-produced mozzarella.

» If desired, grill the chicken in a grill pan or contact grill.

RED WINE–BRAISED BEEF & PEPPERS

Come home when cooking Red Wine–Braised Beef and Peppers in your slow cooker and the most delicious aroma will greet you. The juices are especially good, and you may want to accompany this dish with cooked noodles, rice, couscous, mashed potatoes, or crusty bread.

1 TABLESPOON VEGETABLE OIL

2 BONELESS BEEF CHUCK FLAT-IRON STEAKS, ABOUT 1 POUND EACH

1 MEDIUM ONION, SLICED

1 CUP SLICED BUTTON MUSHROOMS

1 LARGE RED BELL PEPPER, CUT INTO ¼-INCH-THICK STRIPS

1 TEASPOON DRY MINCED GARLIC

½ TEASPOON ITALIAN SEASONING

½ TEASPOON KOSHER SALT, PLUS MORE AS NEEDED

COARSELY GROUND BLACK PEPPER

1 TABLESPOON BALSAMIC VINEGAR

¼ CUP REDUCED-SODIUM BEEF BROTH

SERVES 4 TO 6

Spray a 4-quart slow cooker with nonstick spray.

Heat the oil in a 12-inch skillet over medium-high heat. Brown the beef, one piece at a time, until the meat is well browned, turning it to brown both sides. Place the browned beef in the slow cooker.

Add the onion to the drippings in the skillet and cook over medium heat, stirring frequently, for 3 minutes. Add the mushrooms and cook, stirring frequently and scraping up any bits of beef left in the skillet, for 4 to 5 minutes, or until the onions are tender and the moisture has evaporated from the mushrooms. Place the onions and mushrooms over the beef in the slow cooker, then top with the bell pepper strips. Sprinkle with the garlic, Italian seasoning, salt, and pepper to taste. Add the balsamic vinegar. Pour the broth and wine over the top.

Cover and cook on low for 6 to 8 hours or until the meat is tender.

¼ CUP DRY RED WINE

2 TABLESPOONS ALL-PURPOSE
  FLOUR

2 TABLESPOONS COLD WATER

1 TABLESPOON MINCED
  FRESH THYME LEAVES, PLUS
  ADDITIONAL THYME SPRIGS
  (OPTIONAL), FOR SERVING

Transfer the beef and vegetables to a deep platter, cover, and keep warm.

Turn the slow cooker to high. Season the drippings with additional salt and pepper, if desired. Combine the flour and the cold water in a small bowl, blending with a fork until smooth. Blend the flour-water paste and minced thyme into the drippings. Cover and cook on high for 15 to 20 minutes, or until the liquid boils and thickens slightly. Spoon the sauce over the meat.

Serve warm, garnished with sprigs of fresh thyme, if desired.

TIPS:

» Browning the meat, onions, and mushrooms adds a wonderful flavor, but when time is short on a busy morning, this step can be eliminated. Place the onion in the slow cooker first, then add the beef, top with the mushrooms, and proceed as directed above.

» Do you have a larger slow cooker? This recipe can also be prepared in a 6-quart slow cooker.

» The best cuts of beef to cook in a slow cooker are the less tender cuts, such as those from the chuck, rump, or bottom round. If your store does not sell chuck flat-iron steaks, substitute about 2 pounds chuck roast or Swiss steak, cut about 1 inch thick, or a roast such as a boneless rump roast.

BBQ PULLED PORK

We were both born and raised in Kansas City, home of world-famous barbecue. Imagine our delight when we discovered hometown recipes that don't require hours and hours of smoke and fire. You will love this, too, for the slow cooker means you can come home after a busy day and have dinner ready with little effort.

1 MEDIUM ONION, THINLY SLICED

3 POUNDS BONELESS OR 4 TO
  5 POUNDS BONE-IN PORK
  SHOULDER (ALSO KNOWN AS
  PORK BUTT), TWINE OR NETTING
  REMOVED

1 TABLESPOON PAPRIKA

2 TEASPOONS DRY MINCED
  GARLIC

2 TABLESPOONS PACKED BROWN
  SUGAR

1 TABLESPOON DRY MUSTARD

1 TABLESPOON KOSHER SALT

1 TEASPOON COARSELY GROUND
  BLACK PEPPER

½ CUP BEER

1 CUP PREPARED BARBECUE SAUCE

SERVES 8

Spray a 4-quart slow cooker with nonstick spray.

Place the onion slices in the bottom of the slow cooker. Place the pork on top of the onion.

Mix together the paprika, garlic, brown sugar, dry mustard, salt, and pepper in a small bowl. Take 1 tablespoon of the beer, add it to the spices, and stir to form a paste. Pat the spice mixture all over the sides and top of the pork. Drizzle the remaining beer around the sides of the pork.

Cover and cook on low for 7 to 9 hours. Carefully remove the meat and onions from the slow cooker and place it on a tray to cool slightly. Pour the liquid that has collected in the slow cooker into a deep bowl and set aside.

Using two forks, shred the meat into bite-size pieces and return it to the slow cooker. Return the cooked onion to the meat, if desired. Stir in the barbecue sauce. Cover and cook on low for 30 minutes more, or until heated through.

TIPS:

» We recommend using dry minced garlic when you are slow cooking. The garlic flavor will not fade and will nicely flavor the foods in the slow cooker. We do not recommend this type of garlic for quick cooking on the stove—that's the time to use fresh garlic.

» This recipe makes delicious sandwiches. Spoon the barbecue filling onto toasted hamburger buns.

» BBQ Pulled Pork is great to freeze, then just thaw, heat, and serve on a busy evening. Spoon about two servings of the cooked meat into a freezer container. Moisten the meat lightly with a few tablespoons of the reserved cooking liquid. Cover, label, and freeze the containers. When ready to serve, allow the meat to thaw in the refrigerator overnight or place it in the refrigerator before you leave for work that day, then when ready to serve, heat it in the microwave until steaming hot.

» Do you have a larger slow cooker? This recipe can also be prepared in a 6-quart slow cooker.

PULLED PORK CARNITAS

Carnitas is the Mexican word for "little meats." Carnitas is usually served as a filling for tacos or burritos.

1 MEDIUM YELLOW ONION, THINLY SLICED

3 POUNDS BONELESS OR 4 TO 5 POUNDS BONE-IN PORK SHOULDER (ALSO KNOWN AS PORK BUTT), TWINE OR NETTING REMOVED

2 CHIPOTLE PEPPERS IN ADOBO SAUCE, SEEDED AND FINELY CHOPPED

1 TABLESPOON ADOBO SAUCE FROM CHIPOTLE PEPPERS IN ADOBO SAUCE

1 TABLESPOON WORCESTERSHIRE SAUCE

2 TEASPOONS DRY MINCED GARLIC

1 TEASPOON DRIED OREGANO LEAVES

1 TEASPOON CHILI POWDER

2 TEASPOONS KOSHER SALT

1 (14.5-OUNCE) CAN PETITE DICED TOMATOES, WITH LIQUID

CORN TORTILLAS, WARMED, FOR SERVING

CRUMBLED QUESO FRESCO OR SHREDDED MEXICAN-BLEND CHEESE, FOR SERVING

1 AVOCADO, PITTED, PEELED, AND DICED, FOR SERVING

SALSA, FOR SERVING

SERVES 8

Spray a 4-quart slow cooker with nonstick spray.

Place the onion slices in the bottom of the slow cooker and place the pork on top of the onion.

Mix together the chipotle peppers, adobo sauce, Worcestershire sauce, garlic, oregano, chili powder, and salt in a small bowl. Spread this mixture on the sides and top of the pork. Spoon the diced tomatoes and their juices around the pork.

Cover and cook on low for 7 to 9 hours. Carefully remove the meat and onions from the slow cooker and place it on a tray to cool slightly. Pour the liquid that has collected in the slow cooker into a deep bowl and set aside.

Using two forks, shred the meat into bite-size pieces and return it to the slow cooker. Return the cooked onion to the meat, if desired.

Skim the fat from the reserved cooking liquid and place it in a 1-quart saucepan. Boil the liquid over medium-high heat, uncovered, until it has reduced to a syruplike consistency, 5 to 10 minutes. Pour the desired amount of this reduced liquid over the pork and heat on low or high setting just until heated through.

To serve, spoon the pork onto warm corn tortillas. Top as desired with queso fresco, avocado, and salsa.

(continued)

TIPS:

» To heat corn tortillas in the microwave: Drizzle about 3 tablespoons of water over a clean kitchen towel. Wrap the corn tortillas in the towel and place in a zip-top bag—do not seal. Microwave on 50% power for 2 minutes to create a steamy environment and to heat the tortillas through. Carefully unwrap and serve. To heat corn tortillas in a hot skillet: Place corn tortillas in a hot skillet and cook for 15 to 30 seconds per side, or until heated through.

» Like more spice? Substitute 1 (14.5-ounce) can fire-roasted diced tomatoes for the petite diced tomatoes.

» Chipotle peppers in adobo sauce are readily available canned in the Mexican or Latino section of the grocery store. Use what you need for this recipe, then freeze the rest: Spread the peppers, with a little sauce on each, in single layer on a small tray or plate. Freeze for 30 to 60 minutes or until firm. Gather the frozen chile peppers and seal them in a freezer bag, label, and return to the freezer. By freezing them separately first you will be able to remove one at a time from the freezer. For the best flavor, use them within about 6 months.

» Pulled Pork Carnitas is great to freeze, then just thaw, heat, and serve on a busy evening. Spoon about two servings of the cooked meat into a freezer container. Moisten the meat lightly with a few tablespoons of the reduced cooking liquid. Cover, label, and freeze the containers. When ready to serve, allow the meat to thaw in the refrigerator overnight or place in the refrigerator before you leave for work that day, then when ready to serve, heat in the microwave until steaming hot.

» For a more attractive presentation, stir chopped tomatoes or pico de gallo into the cooked meat just before serving.

» Queso fresco is a Mexican fresh white cheese similar to farmer's cheese in texture. It may also be labeled queso blanco. If you cannot find queso fresco in your market, you could substitute feta cheese or shredded Monterey Jack cheese.

» Do you have a large slow cooker? This recipe can also be prepared in a 6-quart slow cooker.

CUBAN SANDWICHES
with PICKLED RED ONIONS

While cafés in Miami are famous for their Cuban sandwiches, you two will quickly become known far and wide for serving the best Cuban sandwiches. Top these sandwiches with pickled onions you made yourself and the flavor will explode. These are perfect to serve when your friends gather at your house to watch a big game or when you invite the neighbors over.

3 POUNDS BONELESS OR 4 TO
  5 POUNDS BONE-IN PORK
  SHOULDER (ALSO KNOWN AS
  PORK BUTT), TWINE OR NETTING
  REMOVED

1½ TABLESPOONS OLIVE OIL

2 TEASPOONS KOSHER SALT

2 TEASPOONS GROUND CUMIN

2 TEASPOONS DRIED OREGANO
  LEAVES

1 TEASPOON COARSELY GROUND
  BLACK PEPPER

¼ TEASPOON RED PEPPER FLAKES

2 TEASPOONS DRY MINCED GARLIC

3 TABLESPOONS FRESH LIME JUICE

2 TABLESPOONS ORANGE JUICE

8 CIABATTA ROLLS OR 1 BAGUETTE

WHOLE-GRAIN DIJON MUSTARD,
  FOR SERVING

SMOKED DELI HAM SLICES, FOR
  SERVING

DILL PICKLE SLICES, FOR SERVING

PICKLED RED ONIONS (SEE RECIPE
  BELOW), FOR SERVING

SWISS CHEESE SLICES, FOR SERVING

SERVES 8

Spray a 4-quart slow cooker with nonstick spray. Make several slits in the pork roast using a paring knife. Place the pork roast in the slow cooker.

Stir together the olive oil, salt, cumin, oregano, black pepper, red pepper flakes, garlic, lime juice, and orange juice in a small bowl. Rub the olive oil mixture over the top and sides of the pork roast.

Cover and cook on low for 7 to 9 hours, or until the meat is very tender.

Carefully remove the meat from the slow cooker and place it on a tray to cool slightly. Pour the liquid that has collected in the slow cooker into a deep bowl and set aside.

Using two forks, shred the meat into bite-size pieces and return it to the slow cooker. Skim the fat from the reserved cooking liquid. Pour about 1 cup of the liquid over the meat. Cover and cook on low for 30 minutes more. (Save the remaining liquid if you plan on freezing leftovers; see Tips, page 26.)

To serve, split the ciabatta rolls or baguette horizontally and spread Dijon on the cut surfaces. Top with the shredded pork, smoked ham, pickles, pickled onions, and Swiss cheese.

(continued)

TIPS:

» If desired, place the sandwiches, open-faced, under the broiler to melt the Swiss cheese. Watch carefully and remove as soon as the cheese begins to melt to avoid burning. Close the sandwiches and serve.

» The shredded pork for Cuban Sandwiches is great to freeze, then just thaw, heat, and serve on a busy evening. Spoon about two servings of the cooked meat into a freezer container. Moisten the meat lightly with a few tablespoons of the reserved cooking liquid. Cover, label, and freeze the containers. When ready to serve, allow the meat to thaw in the refrigerator overnight or place in the refrigerator before you leave for work that day, then when ready to serve, heat in the microwave until steaming hot.

» Do you have a large slow cooker? This recipe can also be prepared in a 6-quart slow cooker.

PICKLED RED ONION

1 MEDIUM RED ONION, THINLY
   SLICED

3 CUPS BOILING WATER

½ TEASPOON GRANULATED SUGAR

½ TEASPOON KOSHER SALT

¾ CUP RICE VINEGAR, WHITE
   VINEGAR, OR APPLE CIDER
   VINEGAR

WHOLE BLACK PEPPERCORNS

1 CLOVE GARLIC

MAKES APPROXIMATELY 1 PINT

Place the onion slices in a sieve. Pour the boiling water over the onion; allow to drain.

Stir together the sugar, salt, and vinegar in a glass 1-pint canning jar. Add the peppercorns and garlic clove. Add the onions to the jar. Let stand at least 30 minutes. Cover and store in the refrigerator for up to 1 month.

MARINARA SAUCE

Once you make—and taste—your own marinara sauce, you will avoid buying those jars of premade sauce. This one will become your favorite! Marinara is one the most versatile sauces you will ever make. Yes, use it on pasta, but think outside of *that* box. It is great on pizza, flatbreads, calzones, panini, and more!

2 TABLESPOONS OLIVE OIL

1 LARGE ONION, DICED

8 CLOVES GARLIC, MINCED

¼ CUP MINCED FRESH FLAT-LEAF
　　PARSLEY

1 TABLESPOON GRANULATED
　　SUGAR

2 TEASPOONS DRIED BASIL LEAVES

1½ TEASPOONS DRIED OREGANO
　　LEAVES

½ TEASPOON KOSHER SALT

½ TEASPOON COARSELY GROUND
　　BLACK PEPPER

2 (28-OUNCE) CANS CRUSHED
　　TOMATOES

1 (6-OUNCE) CAN TOMATO PASTE

½ CUP DRY RED WINE

MAKES ABOUT 9 CUPS

Spray a 4-quart slow cooker with nonstick spray.

Heat the olive oil in a 12-inch skillet over medium-high heat. Add the onions and cook, stirring frequently, for 5 to 6 minutes, or until the onion is tender but not beginning to brown. Add the garlic and cook, stirring, for 30 seconds.

Pour the cooked onions and garlic into the slow cooker. Stir in the remaining ingredients as well as ½ cup water.

Cover and cook on low for 6 to 8 hours.

TIPS:

» Leftovers can be ladled into lidded freezer containers. Cover, label, and freeze for up to 6 months. Thaw it in the refrigerator overnight and you will be able to heat it up on a busy evening in just minutes.

» Prepare and brown meatballs or add frozen meatballs to the sauce and cook as directed above.

» Brown Italian sausage links in olive oil in a 10-inch skillet over medium heat. Add the sausage to the sauce and cook as directed above.

» Do you have a larger slow cooker? This recipe can also be prepared in a 6-quart slow cooker.

TEX-MEX FOUR-BEAN VEGETARIAN CHILI

What is the best part of this chili? The fantastic flavor? The colorful beans and vegetables? The aroma wafting from the slow cooker as you come home after a busy day? Or is it that this thick chili will be equally enjoyed by everyone? All of the above!

½ MEDIUM YELLOW ONION, CHOPPED

1 MEDIUM CARROT, FINELY CHOPPED

1 JALAPEÑO PEPPER, SEEDED AND FINELY CHOPPED

1 (15-OUNCE) CAN BLACK BEANS, RINSED AND DRAINED

1 (15-OUNCE) CAN RED OR DARK RED BEANS, RINSED AND DRAINED

1 (15.8-OUNCE) CAN GREAT NORTHERN BEANS, RINSED AND DRAINED

1 (15-OUNCE) CAN PINTO BEANS, RINSED AND DRAINED

1 (14.5-OUNCE) CAN DICED TOMATOES, WITH LIQUID

1 CUP SALSA

1 (4-OUNCE) CAN CHOPPED GREEN CHILES

1 CUP FROZEN WHOLE KERNEL CORN

3 TABLESPOONS CHILI POWDER

4 TEASPOONS GROUND CUMIN

1 TABLESPOON DRY MINCED GARLIC

KOSHER SALT AND FRESHLY GROUND BLACK PEPPER, TO TASTE

CRUSHED TORTILLA CHIPS (OPTIONAL), FOR SERVING

SHREDDED SHARP CHEDDAR CHEESE (OPTIONAL), FOR SERVING

SERVES 6 TO 8

Spray a 4-quart slow cooker with nonstick spray.

Place the onion, carrot, and jalapeño pepper in the slow cooker. Stir in the beans, tomatoes, salsa, green chilies, and corn. Stir in the chili powder, cumin, garlic, salt, and pepper. Cover and cook on low for 6 to 8 hours.

Ladle the chili into bowls. Top each serving with crushed tortilla chips and shredded cheese, if desired.

TIPS:

» Do you like your chili hot and spicy or milder in flavor? If you wish a spicier flavor, increase the chili powder to 3½ to 4 tablespoons and add ¼ to ½ teaspoon cayenne pepper, or to taste. For a milder chili use mild salsa, begin with ½ of a jalapeño pepper, and reduce the chili powder to 2 tablespoons. Taste the chili during the last 30 minutes and add additional chili powder, cumin, cayenne, or hot sauce, to taste.

» The spicy flavor of the jalapeño pepper is concentrated in the seeds and membranes. For a milder flavor, remove the seeds and membranes. Be sure to use caution when handling chile peppers and thoroughly wash your hands, the cutting board, and the knife after chopping the peppers.

» This chili tastes great when you make it, and tastes great reheated the next day. If you do have too much chili, ladle it into freezer containers, label it, and freeze it for up to 6 months. Thaw it in the refrigerator overnight and you will be able to heat it up and serve hot chili on a busy evening in just minutes.

CUBAN BLACK BEAN SOUP
with FRESH JALAPEÑO SALSA

Is it a soup or a thick, comforting bean dish? It is both! You won't need to find a little café that ladles up black beans, for you can now make the best Cuban Black Bean Soup in your slow cooker in your own kitchen. For extra flavor, top the beans with a spoonful of Fresh Jalapeño Salsa.

BLACK BEAN SOUP:

8 OUNCES DRIED BLACK BEANS

½ MEDIUM ONION, CHOPPED

½ MEDIUM GREEN BELL PEPPER, CHOPPED

1 MEDIUM HAM HOCK, ABOUT 8 OUNCES

2 TEASPOONS DRY MINCED GARLIC

2 TEASPOONS CHILI POWDER

1 TEASPOON GROUND CUMIN

½ TEASPOON KOSHER SALT, PLUS MORE AS NEEDED

¼ TEASPOON FRESHLY GROUND BLACK PEPPER, PLUS MORE AS NEEDED

1 (14.5-OUNCE) CAN VEGETABLE BROTH

2 TABLESPOONS FRESH LIME JUICE

2 TABLESPOONS MINCED FRESH CILANTRO

SERVES 4 TO 6

MAKE THE BLACK BEAN SOUP: Rinse the beans; pick out and discard any shriveled beans or debris. Place the beans in a deep bowl and add 6 cups cold water, or enough water to cover the beans by at least 1 inch. Set aside and allow the beans to soak at room temperature overnight.

Drain the beans and discard the water.

Spray a 4-quart slow cooker with nonstick spray. Place the beans in the slow cooker. Stir in the onion, bell pepper, ham hock, garlic, chili powder, cumin, salt, pepper, broth, and ½ cup water. Cover and cook on low for 8 to 10 hours, or until the beans are very tender.

Stir in the lime juice and cilantro during the last 15 minutes of cooking. Taste and add additional salt and pepper, if desired.

MAKE THE FRESH JALAPEÑO SALSA: Stir together the tomato, jalapeño, cilantro, and lime juice in a small bowl. Season with salt and pepper.

To serve, spoon hot cooked rice into bowls. Ladle the beans over the rice and top with jalapeño salsa.

FRESH JALAPEÑO SALSA:

1 RIPE MEDIUM TOMATO, SEEDED
   AND CHOPPED

1 JALAPEÑO, SEEDED AND
   MINCED

2 TABLESPOONS MINCED FRESH
   CILANTRO

1 TABLESPOON FRESH LIME JUICE

KOSHER SALT AND FRESHLY
   GROUND BLACK PEPPER

HOT COOKED RICE, FOR SERVING

TIPS:

» Cuban Black Bean Soup is often quite thick and is traditionally served over hot cooked rice. If you prefer a thinner soup, add an additional ½ cup water.

» If desired, use a potato masher to partially mash some of the beans just before serving.

» Why soak the beans before cooking? Generally, soak beans to hydrate them, shorten the cooking time, and minimize the sugars in the beans that can cause indigestion. Just cover the black beans with cold water and let them soak at room temperature overnight. In the morning, drain the beans, discarding the soaking water and proceed as the recipe directs. If you are in a hurry, place the beans and cold water in a saucepan, bring to a boil, and cook for 2 minutes, then remove the pan from the heat and allow the beans to soak for 1 to 4 hours, or until soft. Drain and proceed with the recipe.

» Need a quick start in the morning? Soak the beans as directed. Chop the onion and bell pepper, place in a zip-top bag, seal the bag, and refrigerate. Measure the seasonings, cover, and set aside. The next morning, drain the beans and place them in the slow cooker with the already chopped and measured ingredients.

CILANTRO CUMIN CHICKEN CHILI

There is never such a thing as leftover chili. Prepare a comforting pot of this chili and you have a ready-made lunch for the next day, or freeze portions for a quick dinner another night.

2 TABLESPOONS VEGETABLE OIL

1¼ TO 1½ POUNDS BONELESS
   SKINLESS CHICKEN BREASTS
   OR THIGHS, CUT INTO ½-INCH
   CUBES

1 MEDIUM ONION, CHOPPED

1 (15- TO 16-OUNCE) CAN WHITE
   SHOEPEG CORN, DRAINED

1 (4-OUNCE) CAN CHOPPED GREEN
   CHILES

⅓ CUP STORE-BOUGHT SALSA
   VERDE

1 TABLESPOON DRY MINCED
   GARLIC

1 TABLESPOON GROUND CUMIN

2 TEASPOONS DRIED OREGANO
   LEAVES

¼ TEASPOON CAYENNE PEPPER

KOSHER SALT AND FRESHLY
   GROUND BLACK PEPPER

1 (14.5-OUNCE) CAN REDUCED-
   SODIUM CHICKEN BROTH

SERVES 6

Spray a 4-quart slow cooker with nonstick spray.

Heat the oil in a 12-inch skillet over medium-high heat. Add the chicken and cook, stirring frequently, for about 3 minutes, or until the chicken is just beginning to brown. Add the onion and cook, stirring frequently, for 3 minutes, or until the chicken is browned and the onions are tender. Transfer to the slow cooker. Stir in the corn, green chiles, salsa verde, garlic, cumin, oregano, cayenne, and salt and black pepper to taste. Pour in the broth.

Cover and cook on low for 6 to 7 hours. Stir in the beans and cilantro. Cover and cook on low for 30 minutes more.

Ladle into bowls and top each with crushed tortilla chips and cheese. Sprinkle with additional cilantro, if desired.

1 (16-OUNCE) CAN GREAT
  NORTHERN BEANS, RINSED
  AND DRAINED
2 TABLESPOONS MINCED FRESH
  CILANTRO, PLUS ADDITIONAL
  MINCED CILANTRO FOR SERVING
  (OPTIONAL)
CRUSHED TORTILLA CHIPS, FOR
  SERVING
SHREDDED MONTEREY JACK
  CHEESE, FOR SERVING

TIPS:

» What kind of chicken to use? Many people enjoy boneless skinless chicken breasts, yet boneless skinless chicken thighs are especially good—the dark meat is a little more flavorful. Use whichever you prefer or what is on sale.

» We recommend using dry minced garlic when you are slow cooking. The garlic flavor will not fade and will nicely flavor the foods in the slow cooker. We do not recommend this type of garlic for quick cooking on the stove—that's the time to use fresh garlic.

» Shoepeg corn is a variety of sweet, white corn and is available canned. If shoepeg is not available, substitute any other variety of canned white corn or sweet yellow corn or substitute 1½ cups frozen corn, thawed.

» Do you have a larger slow cooker? This recipe can also be prepared in a 6-quart slow cooker.

» When slow cooking, taste the dish just before serving. If you prefer a more highly seasoned chili, stir in additional dried oregano leaves, cumin, or cayenne along with the beans.

» Cilantro Cumin Chicken Chili freezes well, so ladle dinner-size portions into freezer containers, cover, label, and freeze. Set the frozen chili in the refrigerator the night before you want to enjoy it, or even as you race out of the door to work that morning. It will be partially thawed and easy to reheat in the microwave that night.

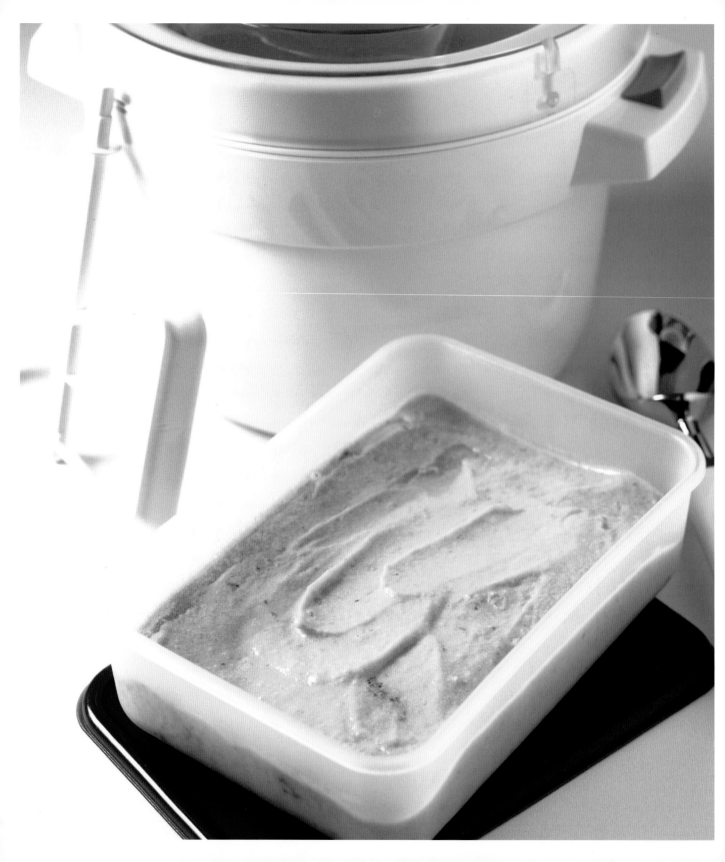

SWEET CREAM MORELLO CHERRY ICE CREAM

Morello cherries, a variety of sour cherries with dark red skin, are not usually available fresh. We find them in jars packed in light syrup in the fruit aisle of Trader Joe's. Since the variety is especially popular in Europe, you could also check with specialty shops that feature European foods. We prefer the tart flavor paired with the sweet cream ice cream. You could substitute maraschino cherries, if you prefer a sweeter flavor.

2 CUPS HEAVY CREAM

¾ CUP GRANULATED SUGAR

DASH OF TABLE SALT

1 TABLESPOON PURE VANILLA
    EXTRACT

1 CUP WHOLE MILK

1 CUP DARK MORELLO CHERRIES
    IN LIGHT SYRUP, DRAINED AND
    HALVED

½ TEASPOON PURE ALMOND
    EXTRACT

MAKES ABOUT 1 QUART

Heat 1 cup of the cream, the sugar, and the salt in a 1-quart saucepan over medium heat, stirring continuously, until the sugar has dissolved. Remove from the heat and stir in the vanilla. Stir in the remaining 1 cup cream and the milk. Cover and chill overnight in the refrigerator.

Transfer the chilled cream mixture to an ice cream maker and process into ice cream according to the manufacturer's directions. Carefully spoon the ice cream into a 2-quart bowl. Fold in the cherries and almond extract. Cover and freeze for 1 hour, or until the desired firmness is reached.

TIPS:

» Stir in ⅓ cup toasted chopped pecans when adding the cherries to the ice cream mixture.

ROSEMARY FOCACCIA

Let that heavy-duty mixer do all of the work while you take all of the credit! This easy Rosemary Focaccia will quickly become a favorite bread for both of you. It is a great accompaniment for a soup, salad, or pasta dish, or you can serve it as an appetizer. You can even split it and make a fantastic sandwich. Be sure to try it with the flavored olive oil dipping sauce noted in the tips, opposite.

2⅔ TO 2¾ CUPS ALL-PURPOSE
  FLOUR

2 TEASPOONS GRANULATED
  SUGAR

½ TEASPOON TABLE SALT

½ TEASPOON ITALIAN SEASONING

1 PACKAGE (2¼ TEASPOONS)
  QUICK-RISING ACTIVE DRY
  YEAST

1 CUP WARM WATER (100 TO 110°F)

3 TABLESPOONS OLIVE OIL,
  PLUS MORE AS NEEDED FOR
  BRUSHING THE LOAF

½ TEASPOON KOSHER SALT OR
  OTHER COARSE SALT, OR TO
  TASTE

2 TABLESPOONS MINCED FRESH
  ROSEMARY

2 TABLESPOONS SHREDDED
  PARMESAN CHEESE

MAKES 1 (10- TO 11-INCH) ROUND LOAF

Combine 1 cup of the flour, the sugar, table salt, Italian seasoning, and yeast in the bowl of a stand mixer fitted with the paddle attachment. Mix on low speed for 30 seconds. Add the water and olive oil. Beat on medium speed for 1 minute.

Add 1 cup of the flour and beat on medium speed for 1 minute.

Change to the dough hook and add ⅔ cup of the flour. Knead on low speed for 30 seconds or until all of the flour is blended into the dough. Increase to high speed and knead for 3 minutes. Stop and check to see if the dough is very sticky. If it is, add the remaining flour. Beat on high speed for 3 minutes, or until the dough is smooth and elastic.

Lightly oil a large bowl and turn the dough into the bowl. Turn the dough over to lightly coat it in the oil. Cover with a clean cloth and set aside in a warm, draft-free spot for 1 hour, or until the dough has doubled in volume.

Punch down the dough. Cover and let rest for 10 minutes.

Preheat the oven to 400°F. Lightly oil a 12-inch pizza pan or 15 x 10-inch baking sheet.

Turn the dough onto the prepared pan. Using your fingers, press the dough into a 10- to 11-inch round. Brush the top of the dough with olive oil. Sprinkle the dough with kosher salt and rosemary. Using your fingers press lightly to be sure the rosemary adheres to the dough. For a classic dimpled look, use the tips of your fingers to make indentations all over the dough. Cover with a cloth and set aside to rise for about 30 minutes, or until doubled in volume.

Bake for 15 minutes, or until set and very lightly brown, then sprinkle with Parmesan and bake for 2 to 3 minutes more, or until golden brown. Transfer to a wire rack to cool slightly. Cut into wedges and serve warm the same day.

TIPS:

» Season the top of the loaf with a generous sprinkle of freshly ground black pepper. Add the pepper when sprinkling with the salt and the rosemary.

» Omit the Parmesan cheese or substitute shredded Asiago cheese.

» Serve warm wedges of Rosemary Focaccia with olive oil seasoned with herbs as a dipping sauce. For a quick, easy version, stir together ¼ cup olive oil, 2 tablespoons Italian seasoning, ½ teaspoon kosher salt, ½ teaspoon garlic powder, and ¼ teaspoon red pepper flakes. Let stand for 5 to 10 minutes, then dip away.

» Use the Rosemary Focaccia to make great sandwiches. Split the bread in half horizontally and top with your favorite sliced deli meat and cheese. Try it with a delicious artichoke mayonnaise: Combine ¼ cup chopped marinated artichoke hearts, drained, ¼ cup mayonnaise, and ½ teaspoon garlic powder. Stir together and spread over the split bread. Top with any desired meat and cheese for a tasty sandwich.

TOASTED PECAN DULCE DE LECHE WAFFLES

Saturdays are perfect for sleeping late and relaxing. Then, indulge and make Toasted Pecan Dulce de Leche Waffles for a late brunch.

TOASTED PECAN WAFFLES:

1 CUP ALL-PURPOSE FLOUR

1 TABLESPOON GRANULATED
  SUGAR

½ TEASPOON BAKING POWDER

¼ TEASPOON BAKING SODA

¼ TEASPOON TABLE SALT

2 LARGE EGGS

¾ CUP BUTTERMILK

2 TABLESPOONS UNSALTED
  BUTTER, MELTED

⅓ CUP CHOPPED PECANS,
  TOASTED

DULCE DE LECHE SYRUP:

½ CUP DULCE DE LECHE

2 TABLESPOONS ORANGE JUICE

½ TEASPOON GROUND
  CINNAMON

SERVES 2

MAKE THE WAFFLES: Whisk together the flour, sugar, baking powder, baking soda, and salt in a large bowl. Set aside.

Lightly beat the eggs in a small bowl. Whisk in the buttermilk and melted butter. Pour the buttermilk mixture over the dry ingredients and stir until combined. Stir in the pecans.

Preheat a waffle maker. Spray the grids with nonstick spray. Pour about 1 cup of the batter evenly over the lower grid. Close and bake for 2 to 3 minutes, or until the light indicates the waffle is done.

MAKE THE SYRUP: Combine the dulce de leche, orange juice, and cinnamon in a small microwave-safe glass bowl. Microwave on high for 45 to 60 seconds, or until hot, stirring halfway through. Stir well.

Serve the warm syrup over the waffles.

TIPS:

» How large is a waffle and how much batter should you use? Each waffle maker varies in size and depth of the waffles. Check the information that came with your waffle maker or the manufacturer's website to see what the manufacturer recommends, and your waffles will come out perfect—fully filled but not overflowing down the outside. This recipe makes about 2 cups of batter.

» Toasting pecans intensifies their flavor. To toast the pecans, spread them in a single layer on a baking sheet. Toast in a preheated 350°F oven for 5 to 7 minutes, or until lightly toasted.

» Buttermilk adds a great tangy flavor, but if you don't have buttermilk on hand, stir 2¼ teaspoons lemon juice or white vinegar into ¾ cup milk. Let the mixture stand for 5 to 10 minutes, or until thickened. Use as directed in the recipe.

» Add some fruit, if you desire. Top the waffles with sliced apples, pears, peaches, bananas, or blueberries, then drizzle with the dulce de leche syrup. For added flavor, cook apple, pear, or peach slices in 1 tablespoon unsalted butter in a 1-quart saucepan over medium-low heat, stirring frequently, for 3 to 5 minutes, or just until the fruit is tender.

» Dulce de leche is a thick, sweet caramel and is now readily available canned or bottled. Look for it in larger grocery stores, shelved with the Latin American foods or with the condensed milk.

WEEKNIGHT
DINNERS

SAUTÉED CHICKEN CUTLETS

Master this and you become an expert at fast, flavorful cooking—dinner will never be more than minutes away. Quickly cook the chicken using this recipe, then finish it with one of the sauces on pages 48 to 53.

2 BONELESS SKINLESS CHICKEN
    BREASTS, ABOUT 6 OUNCES
    EACH
1 TABLESPOON VEGETABLE OIL,
    CANOLA OIL, OR OLIVE OIL
KOSHER SALT AND FRESHLY
    GROUND BLACK PEPPER

SERVES 2

Pound the chicken breasts between sheets of plastic wrap until the chicken is about ½ inch thick.

Heat the oil in a 12-inch skillet over medium-high heat. Place the chicken in a single layer in the skillet. Season the chicken with salt and pepper.

Cook the chicken for about 3 minutes, or until browned on the bottom. Turn the chicken and cook for 3 to 5 minutes more, or until the chicken is no longer pink inside and a meat thermometer inserted into the center registers 165°F.

Transfer the chicken to a plate, cover with aluminum foil, and let rest for 5 minutes before serving.

TIPS:

» Pat the chicken dry with a paper towel before cooking to ensure better, more even browning.

» While the chicken rests after cooking, quickly prepare one of the sauces on pages 48 to 53. Some of our favorites for chicken are the French Dijon Sauce (page 49), Marsala Sauce (page 50), and the Ginger Sauce (page 52).

» Be sure that the skillet and oil are both hot before adding the chicken. Hot oil will shimmer and a pinch of flour will sizzle when sprinkled in the oil.

(continued)

TIPS:

» Pounding the chicken makes it thinner, but also makes the chicken breast even in thickness so it cooks more evenly. If not pounded, a chicken breast has a thicker center and thin edges so the edges overcook before the center is done.

» Chicken must be cooked until done, but if overcooked, the meat becomes dry. Use a meat thermometer to ensure that it is perfectly cooked—done yet moist.

» Cooked chicken or any meat will taste more moist if allowed to rest for about 5 minutes after cooking and before serving. This is the perfect time to go ahead and make a quick sauce. If you are making a sauce that takes a little longer to cook, preheat the oven to 200°F, place the cooked chicken in an ovenproof dish, cover, and place in the oven to keep warm.

» Do you want a crispier coating? Sprinkle about ½ cup all-purpose flour in a shallow dish and season it with salt and pepper. After pounding the chicken, dip the pieces in the flour mixture, turning to coat them evenly. Increase the oil to 2 tablespoons and cook as directed.

PAN SAUTÉED BEEF

From everyday dinners to more elegant fare, beef quickly cooked in a hot skillet is the basis of many wonderful meals. This quick method also makes it easy to enjoy beef even if you don't have access to an outside grill.

1 TABLESPOON VEGETABLE OIL OR
    CANOLA OIL
½ POUND TENDER BEEF
    (TENDERLOIN, RIB EYE, STRIP,
    SIRLOIN, TOP ROUND, FLAT-
    IRON, OR CUBED STEAK,
    SEE TIPS BELOW), CUT ABOUT
    ½ INCH THICK
KOSHER SALT AND FRESHLY
    GROUND BLACK PEPPER

SERVES 2

Heat the oil in a 12-inch skillet over medium-high heat. Add the steak and cook for 2 minutes, or until browned. Turn the steak to brown the second side and cook for 1 to 2 minutes more, or until browned and a meat thermometer inserted in the center registers 145°F for medium-rare or 160°F for medium.

Transfer the steak to a plate. Season with salt and pepper. Cover with aluminum foil and let rest for 5 minutes before serving.

TIPS:

» Pat the beef dry with a paper towel before cooking to ensure better, more even browning.

» If you're cooking the beef on a grill pan, contact grill, or multi grill, omit the oil.

» While the beef rests after cooking, quickly prepare one of the sauces on pages 48 to 53. Some of our favorites for beef are the Red Wine Reduction (page 48) and the Bourbon Sauce (page 53).

» Cuts such as sirloin, top round, and flat-iron steaks may be available cut about ½ inch thick. Do you want to cook a thicker cut of beef? Combine a quick sauté in the skillet with a few minutes roasting in the oven. Preheat the oven to 450°F and select a heavy, oven-safe skillet such as a cast-iron or enameled cast-iron skillet. Cook the beef as directed until browned on the first side. Turn the beef, then carefully place the hot skillet into the preheated oven. Roast for 3 to 5 minutes, or until a meat thermometer inserted in the center registers 145°F for medium-rare or 160°F for medium. Remove the meat from the skillet and place on a plate. Let the meat rest as directed above.

QUICK & CLASSIC SAUTÉED PORK

While the pork rests after cooking, quickly prepare one of the sauces on pages 48 to 53. Some of our favorites for pork are the Salsa Verde Sauce (page 51) and the French Dijon Sauce (page 49).

1 TABLESPOON VEGETABLE OIL,
CANOLA OIL, OR OLIVE OIL
2 BONELESS PORK CHOPS, ABOUT
¾ INCH THICK
KOSHER SALT AND FRESHLY
GROUND BLACK PEPPER

SERVES 2

Heat the oil in a 12-inch skillet over medium-high heat. Add the chops and season with salt and pepper. Cook, uncovered, for about 3 minutes, or until the chops are browned. Turn and cook for 3 to 5 minutes more, or until the second side is browned and a meat thermometer inserted in the center registers 145°F.

Transfer the chops to a plate, cover with aluminum foil, and let rest for 5 minutes before serving.

TIPS:

» Pat the pork dry with a paper towel before cooking to ensure better, more even browning.

» The minimum safe internal temperature for pork is 145°F. While safe to eat, the meat will still look quite pink. If you prefer the meat a little more done, cook until the internal temperature is about 155°F. While your mom or grandma may have recommended that pork never be served pink, that is no longer necessary, according to USDA guidelines for safe cooking. In fact, pork is now so lean that if overcooked, it will taste dry.

» How thick is a chop? Chops are tender cuts from the loin and may be available as boneless or bone-in. Chops may be cut thin, ½ to ¾ inch thick or up to about 1½ inches thick. In general, the thinner the chop, the higher the heat can be and the more quickly it will cook. A thicker chop should be cooked more slowly over more moderate heat so it cooks evenly all the way through.

» What is a cutlet? A cutlet is a very thin boneless piece cut from the sirloin or tenderloin. They are very tender and cook quite quickly. This cut is commonly available in some markets, yet is more difficult to find in others. To cut your own, begin with a pork tenderloin and slice the meat crosswise, about 1 inch thick. Place the slices between sheets of plastic wrap and pound the meat until very thin, ¼ to ½ inch thick. Cook the cutlets as directed for the chops, but reduce the cooking time to about 2 minutes per side, or until the cutlets are browned and the meat is just slightly pink.

RED WINE REDUCTION SAUCE

Red Wine Reduction is a seductive sauce that transforms meat, especially beef, into a restaurant specialty. Follow the tip below if making a wine sauce for chicken.

1 TABLESPOON VEGETABLE OIL

1 SHALLOT, MINCED

¾ CUP DRY RED WINE

½ CUP REDUCED-SODIUM BEEF
    BROTH

KOSHER SALT AND FRESHLY
    GROUND BLACK PEPPER

1 TABLESPOON UNSALTED BUTTER

1 TABLESPOON MINCED FRESH
    THYME LEAVES, ROSEMARY, OR
    FLAT-LEAF PARSLEY

SAUTÉED MEAT OF YOUR CHOICE
    (PAGES 42, 45, AND 46)

MAKES ABOUT ⅔ CUP

Heat the oil in a skillet (you can use the same skillet you used to cook the meat) over medium heat. Add the shallot and cook, stirring frequently, for 2 minutes, or until the shallot is tender. Stir in the wine and broth. Season with salt and pepper. Cook, uncovered, stirring frequently, for 5 to 8 minutes, or until the liquid has reduced by about half.

Whisk in the butter and cook, whisking continuously, until the butter melts. Stir in the herbs and cook for 30 seconds. Spoon the sauce over the meat.

TIPS:

» The flavor of a red wine reduction makes it especially good on steaks or any piece of beef. It is also good on lamb, but if made with beef broth and red wine, it may overpower chicken. For chicken, substitute chicken broth and dry white wine.

» What is a shallot? A shallot is a member of the onion family, but it is known for its mild flavor that has hints of both garlic and onion. In appearance, it may remind you of a large garlic clove for the head has multiple cloves (often two of them), with each clove covered with papery skin. As this recipe lists one shallot, use just one of the cloves of the shallot, peel away the papery skin, and mince it finely.

FRENCH DIJON SAUCE

The few ingredients in this sauce meld together perfectly and complement any cutlet, especially pork or chicken.

½ CUP DRY WHITE WINE

¾ CUP LOW-SODIUM CHICKEN
BROTH

KOSHER SALT AND FRESHLY
GROUND BLACK PEPPER

½ CUP HEAVY CREAM

1 TABLESPOON WHOLE-GRAIN
DIJON MUSTARD

SAUTÉED MEAT OF YOUR CHOICE
(PAGES 42, 45, AND 46)

MINCED FRESH FLAT-LEAF PARSLEY
(OPTIONAL), FOR SERVING

MAKES ABOUT 1½ CUPS

In a skillet (you can use the same skillet you used to cook the meat), combine the wine and chicken broth and season with salt and pepper. Bring to a boil over medium heat, then reduce the heat to maintain a simmer and cook, stirring occasionally, for 5 to 8 minutes. Stir the cream into the broth and bring the sauce to a boil, stirring continuously. Simmer for 3 to 5 minutes, or until thickened, stirring frequently. Whisk in the mustard and cook until the sauce is heated through and smooth. Spoon the sauce over the meat. If desired, sprinkle with minced parsley.

TIPS:

» Substitute smooth Dijon mustard for whole-grain Dijon mustard, if desired.

» This is an ideal sauce to use if you are cooking a thicker (1- to 1½-inch) chop or cut of meat. Brown the meat on one side, as directed in the recipe. Turn the meat and add the wine and broth, then season with salt and pepper. Heat until the liquid boils, reduce the heat to maintain a simmer, and cook for 5 to 8 minutes, or until the meat is done. Transfer the meat to a platter with shallow sides; cover with aluminum foil to keep warm. Add the cream to the skillet and bring the sauce to a boil. Continue as directed above.

MARSALA SAUCE

No valet parking or restaurant menu is needed. This sauce will elevate home cooking to restaurant-fare quality any day of the week.

1 TABLESPOON OLIVE OIL

4 OUNCES BUTTON MUSHROOMS,
   SLICED

1 CLOVE GARLIC, MINCED

1 TABLESPOON ALL-PURPOSE
   FLOUR

½ CUP REDUCED-SODIUM
   CHICKEN BROTH

½ CUP MARSALA

SAUTÉED MEAT OF YOUR CHOICE
   (PAGES 42, 45, AND 46)

MAKES ABOUT ¾ CUP

Heat the oil in a skillet (you can use the same skillet you used to cook the meat) over medium heat. Add the mushrooms and cook, stirring frequently, until the mushrooms are tender and the liquid evaporates, 4 to 6 minutes. Add the garlic and cook for 30 seconds. Sprinkle the mushroom-garlic mixture with the flour and stir to blend thoroughly. Gradually stir in the chicken broth and marsala. Cook, stirring continuously, until thick and well blended, about 4 to 6 minutes. Spoon the sauce over the meat or chicken.

TIPS:

» Marsala wine is one of Italy's most famous wines and is known for its rich, smoky flavor. No marsala on hand? No worries. You could substitute a dry sherry.

» Restaurants often serve a cutlet topped with marsala sauce with pasta. Follow their lead for a great meal.

» If you would like additional sauce to serve over your cutlet and pasta, feel free to double the recipe.

SALSA VERDE SAUCE

Begin with prepared salsa verde from the pantry, then quickly transform it into a richly flavored sauce that is perfect on chicken or any meat cut.

1 TABLESPOON VEGETABLE OIL

¼ CUP CHOPPED ONION

1 CLOVE GARLIC, MINCED

½ CUP REDUCED-SODIUM
   CHICKEN BROTH

½ CUP STORE-BOUGHT SALSA
   VERDE

1 TABLESPOON FRESH LIME JUICE

½ TEASPOON GROUND CUMIN

KOSHER SALT AND FRESHLY
   GROUND BLACK PEPPER

SAUTÉED MEAT OF YOUR CHOICE
   (PAGES 42, 45, AND 46)

2 TABLESPOONS MINCED FRESH
   CILANTRO (OPTIONAL), FOR
   SERVING

¼ CUP SHREDDED MONTEREY
   JACK CHEESE (OPTIONAL),
   FOR SERVING

MAKES ABOUT ¾ CUP

Heat the oil in a skillet (you can use the same skillet you used to cook the meat) over medium heat. Add the onion and cook, stirring frequently, for 3 minutes, or until the onion is tender. Add the garlic and cook for 30 seconds. Stir in the broth and cook, stirring frequently, until the broth comes to a boil. Reduce the heat to maintain a simmer and cook, uncovered, stirring occasionally, for 5 to 8 minutes, or until the sauce has reduced by about half. Stir in the salsa verde, lime juice, cumin, and salt and pepper to taste. Bring the sauce to a simmer.

Spoon the sauce over the meat. Serve sprinkled with cilantro and cheese, if desired.

TIPS:

» If serving the sauce on beef, substitute beef broth for chicken broth.

» The flavor of salsa verde varies with the brand. If you are unsure of the flavor, stir in ¼ teaspoon cumin. Taste and add the remaining ¼ teaspoon cumin if a more flavorful sauce is preferred.

GINGER SAUCE

This Ginger Sauce is full of flavor, yet is just subtle enough that it does not overpower the meat or the rest of the meal.

½ CUP REDUCED-SODIUM
   CHICKEN BROTH
2 TABLESPOONS WHITE WINE
   VINEGAR
2 TABLESPOONS REDUCED-SODIUM
   SOY SAUCE
1½ TEASPOONS PEELED, MINCED
   FRESH GINGER
1 TEASPOON GRANULATED SUGAR
⅛ TEASPOON RED PEPPER FLAKES
KOSHER SALT AND FRESHLY
   GROUND BLACK PEPPER
2 TABLESPOONS COLD WATER
2 TEASPOONS CORNSTARCH
1 TABLESPOON VEGETABLE OIL
SAUTÉED MEAT OF YOUR CHOICE
   (PAGES 42, 45, AND 46)
1 SCALLION, SLICED, FOR SERVING

MAKES ABOUT ½ CUP

Stir together the chicken broth, vinegar, soy sauce, ginger, sugar, red pepper flakes, and salt and black pepper to taste in a small bowl. Set aside.

Stir together the cold water and cornstarch in a small bowl. Set aside.

Heat a skillet (you can use the same skillet you used to cook the meat) over medium heat. Pour the broth-ginger mixture into the skillet and cook, stirring continuously, until hot and bubbly. Stir the cornstarch-water mixture, then pour the mixture into the skillet. Cook, stirring continuously, until the sauce is thickened and bubbling. Spoon the sauce over the meat. Sprinkle with the scallion.

TIPS:

» Do you like it spicy? If so, increase the red pepper flakes to ¼ teaspoon.

» Ginger, in this recipe, is the knobby root that is readily available at most grocery stores. Do not use dry ground ginger. To prepare the fresh ginger, peel off the tough outer skin, but don't waste too much for the ginger just under the skin is very flavorful. One easy way to remove the skin is to scrape it off using the tip of a spoon. Once the skin is gone, grate the ginger needed for the recipe. If you have a larger piece of ginger than is needed, wrap it tightly and freeze it for up to 6 months. You can then slice off what you need and return the rest to the freezer.

BOURBON SAUCE

Who knew that everyday ingredients that you most likely have on hand could blend together to add a flavor punch to your dinner menu? This Bourbon Sauce is especially suited to beef, chicken, or salmon.

½ CUP BOURBON

3 TABLESPOONS PACKED BROWN
   SUGAR

1 TABLESPOON WHITE WINE
   VINEGAR

1 TABLESPOON WORCESTERSHIRE
   SAUCE

3 TABLESPOONS REDUCED-SODIUM
   SOY SAUCE

2 CLOVES GARLIC, MINCED

½ TEASPOON COARSELY GROUND
   BLACK PEPPER

SAUTÉED MEAT OF YOUR CHOICE
   (PAGES 42, 45, AND 46)

MAKES ABOUT ½ CUP

Stir together the bourbon, brown sugar, vinegar, Worcestershire sauce, soy sauce, garlic, and pepper in a 1-quart saucepan. Bring to a boil over medium heat, stirring occasionally. Reduce the heat to maintain a simmer and cook, uncovered, stirring occasionally, for 5 to 8 minutes, or until the mixture has reduced by half. Spoon the sauce over the meat.

TIPS:

» For a New Orleans–style Bourbon Sauce, stir in 1 to 2 tablespoons toasted chopped pecans just before serving.

KOREAN BBQ STEAK & VEGETABLE BOWLS

Don't sacrifice flavor or nutrition just because you need to get dinner on the table quickly. Korean BBQ Steak and Vegetable Bowls make dinnertime sizzle with flavor in no time.

3 TABLESPOONS REDUCED-SODIUM
    SOY SAUCE

1 TABLESPOON DARK SESAME OIL

2 CLOVES GARLIC, MINCED

1 TABLESPOON PEELED, MINCED
    FRESH GINGER

1 TEASPOON PACKED BROWN
    SUGAR

1/8 TEASPOON RED PEPPER FLAKES

1/2 POUND BEEF SIRLOIN OR TOP
    ROUND

2 CUPS VEGETABLES (SEE TIPS,
    PAGE 56)

HOT COOKED RICE (OPTIONAL),
    FOR SERVING

1 SCALLION, SLICED, FOR SERVING

SERVES 2

Mix together the soy sauce, sesame oil, garlic, ginger, brown sugar, and red pepper flakes in a small bowl. Drizzle 1 to 1½ tablespoons of this mixture over the steak and brush to coat both sides evenly.

Stir together the vegetables and 1 to 1½ tablespoons of the soy sauce mixture in a large bowl. Set the remaining soy sauce mixture aside.

Preheat a grill to medium high or allow the coals to burn down to white ash.

Grill the steak, uncovered, over direct heat for 6 minutes. Turn the meat and grill on the second side for 5 to 7 minutes, or until a meat thermometer inserted into the center registers 145°F for medium-rare or 160°F for medium. Remove steak from the grill, cover with aluminum foil, and let rest for 5 to 10 minutes.

Arrange the vegetables on the grill grate. Grill the vegetables for 7 to 10 minutes, or until they are tender as desired, turning to cook evenly.

Thinly slice the steak. Cut the vegetables into bite-size pieces. Toss together the cooked beef and vegetables in a serving bowl.

To serve, spoon rice, if desired, into two individual serving bowls. Spoon the meat and vegetables over the rice. Drizzle the remaining soy sauce mixture evenly over the meat and vegetables in the bowls. Garnish with the scallion.

(continued)

TIPS:

» If you have a larger grill and you and your spouse want to work as a team, grill the meat simultaneously with the vegetables, placing the meat on one side of the grill and the vegetables on the other. If the grill you are using has an open grate design, place the vegetables on a finer mesh grill grate or in a vegetable grill basket (vegetable grill baskets are commonly sold at kitchen stores).

» If desired, grill the meat and vegetables in a grill pan or contact grill.

» What vegetables should you choose for this recipe? Select red bell pepper, cut into ½-inch strips; zucchini or yellow squash, sliced crosswise about ½ inch thick; button mushrooms, sliced; red onion, sliced ½ inch thick; large broccoli florets; or a combination of vegetables, as desired. Select your favorites from what you have on hand. For quick preparation and no waste, check what vegetables are offered already trimmed and cleaned on the salad bar or in the produce section at your grocery store.

» Scallions or green onions? At some grocery stores, you may find it impossible to purchase green onions, while in other parts of the country, you may never find a scallion. While there is a slight difference between a green onion, which is an immature or spring onion, and a scallion, the names—and the vegetable—are used interchangeably and different terms are preferred in different regions of the country.

THAI-SPICED BEEF & GREENS

Quick, one-dish meals have never tasted this good! Stir-fry dishes, like this Thai-Spiced Beef and Greens, cook very quickly, so be sure to assemble all of the ingredients before beginning to cook. You two will be out of the kitchen in a flash so you can enjoy the evening together.

½ CUP REDUCED-SODIUM BEEF
   BROTH
3 TABLESPOONS CREAMY PEANUT
   BUTTER
2 TABLESPOONS REDUCED-SODIUM
   SOY SAUCE
1 TABLESPOON RICE VINEGAR
2 TEASPOONS GRANULATED
   SUGAR
1½ TEASPOONS DARK SESAME OIL
2 TEASPOONS PEELED, MINCED
   FRESH GINGER
½ TEASPOON SRIRACHA, OR
   ¼ TEASPOON CAYENNE PEPPER
2 TABLESPOONS VEGETABLE OIL
½ POUND BEEF SIRLOIN, TOP
   ROUND, OR FLANK STEAK, VERY
   THINLY SLICED ACROSS THE
   GRAIN INTO 2 X ⅛-INCH STRIPS
½ MEDIUM RED BELL PEPPER,
   THINLY SLICED
1½ CUPS FRESH TRIMMED
   SPINACH LEAVES, TORN INTO
   PIECES
HOT COOKED JASMINE OR LONG-
   GRAIN RICE, FOR SERVING
MINCED FRESH CILANTRO OR
   SLICED SCALLIONS (OPTIONAL),
   FOR SERVING

SERVES 2

Stir together the broth, peanut butter, soy sauce, rice vinegar, sugar, sesame oil, ginger, and Sriracha in a small bowl. Set aside.

Heat the oil in a 12-inch skillet or wok over medium-high heat. Add half of the beef and cook, stirring quickly, for about 2 minutes, or until the beef is well browned. Remove the beef from the skillet, leaving the drippings. Place the beef on a plate and set aside. Repeat with the remaining beef, but do not remove from the skillet.

Return the first batch of beef to the skillet and add the bell pepper. Cook, stirring quickly, for 2 minutes.

Stir the sauce ingredients well, then pour them over the beef and peppers in the skillet. Cook, stirring continuously, for 1 to 2 minutes, or until the sauce is bubbling and smooth. Stir the spinach leaves into the sauce and cook for 1 minute, or until the spinach is just wilted.

Serve over rice. Garnish, if desired, with cilantro or scallions.

TIPS:

» Which cut of beef should you use? Lean boneless beef such as sirloin or top round steak is a great choice. Flank steak or skirt steak are also great choices, but slice the meat very thinly across the grain.

» Freezing meat makes it easier to slice very thinly. Put the meat in the freezer for about 30 minutes, then slice. Or, if already frozen, place the meat in the refrigerator before you leave for work and it will thaw enough to slice when it's time to prepare dinner.

ROASTED VEGETABLE PASTA PRIMAVERA

Roasted Vegetable Pasta Primavera is low in fat and nutritious yet packed with flavor. If you and your spouse work as a team, with one of you preparing the vegetables and one of you cooking the broth and the pasta, you will have dinner on the table in just minutes.

1 MEDIUM CARROT, QUARTERED
    LENGTHWISE AND CUT INTO
    1-INCH PIECES

½ MEDIUM ZUCCHINI OR YELLOW
    SQUASH, HALVED LENGTHWISE
    AND CUT INTO ¼-INCH SLICES

½ MEDIUM ONION, HALVED AND
    SLICED ¼ INCH THICK

½ MEDIUM RED BELL PEPPER,
    HALVED AND SLICED ¼ INCH
    THICK

8 TO 10 ASPARAGUS SPEARS,
    TRIMMED AND CUT IN HALF OR
    THIRDS

2 TABLESPOONS OLIVE OIL

KOSHER SALT AND FRESHLY
    GROUND BLACK PEPPER

1 (14.5-OUNCE) CAN VEGETABLE
    BROTH

1 TABLESPOON FRESH LEMON
    JUICE

SERVES 2

Preheat the oven to 425°F. Line a baking sheet with aluminum foil.

Bring a large pot of salted water to a boil for the pasta.

Place the carrots, zucchini, onion, bell pepper, and asparagus in a zip-top bag. Drizzle the vegetables with the olive oil and season with salt and pepper. Seal the bag and massage to coat the vegetables evenly. Spread the vegetables in a single layer on the prepared baking sheet. Bake for 9 to 11 minutes, or until crisp-tender, stirring midway through baking.

Meanwhile, combine the vegetable broth, lemon juice, Italian seasoning, and garlic in a 1-quart saucepan and bring to a boil over medium-high heat, stirring occasionally. Reduce the heat to maintain a simmer. Cook, uncovered, stirring occasionally, for 10 to 12 minutes, until the broth has reduced to about ⅓ cup.

Meanwhile, cook the pasta in the boiling water according to the package directions. Drain.

Toss together the hot pasta, cherry tomatoes, broth, and vegetables in a large bowl. Sprinkle with Parmesan and basil and serve.

2 TEASPOONS ITALIAN SEASONING

1 CLOVE GARLIC, MINCED

4 OUNCES CAPELLINI (ANGEL
HAIR) OR LINGUINI

½ CUP CHERRY TOMATOES,
QUARTERED

½ CUP SHREDDED PARMESAN
CHEESE, FOR SERVING

2 TABLESPOONS MINCED FRESH
BASIL LEAVES, FOR SERVING

TIPS:

» You can substitute or add more of your favorite vegetables. For example, omit the asparagus and substitute broccoli florets, or add trimmed and halved mushrooms to the other roasted vegetables.

» Why boil the broth? Boiling reduces the liquid and concentrates the flavor. You will find that the reduced broth makes a richly flavored but low-fat sauce for the pasta. Watch carefully so it does not boil dry.

GRILLED CHICKEN CHOPPED SALAD *with* RED WINE VINAIGRETTE

There is no need to go out to a restaurant to enjoy your favorite restaurant-style salad. This recipe is ideal for a great, quick dinner. Do not worry if the weather is inclement or if you do not have an outside grill; you can cook the chicken in a contact grill or in a grill pan and dinner will be ready in just a few minutes.

1 BONELESS SKINLESS CHICKEN
    BREAST, ABOUT 6 OUNCES
¼ CUP OLIVE OIL
3 TABLESPOONS RED WINE
    VINEGAR
1 TEASPOON DIJON MUSTARD
1 CLOVE GARLIC, MINCED
KOSHER SALT AND FRESHLY
    GROUND BLACK PEPPER
2 CUPS CHOPPED ROMAINE
    LETTUCE
⅓ CUP CHERRY OR GRAPE
    TOMATOES, HALVED
⅓ CUP CHOPPED RED BELL PEPPER
¼ CUP CHOPPED MARINATED
    ARTICHOKE HEARTS, DRAINED
¼ CUP CHOPPED RED ONION
¼ TEASPOON ITALIAN SEASONING
SHREDDED PARMESAN CHEESE,
    FOR SERVING

SERVES 2

Pound the chicken breast between sheets of plastic wrap until the chicken is about ½ inch thick. Place the chicken in a zip-top bag.

Whisk together the olive oil, vinegar, mustard, garlic, and salt and pepper to taste in a small bowl. Pour 2 tablespoons of the olive oil mixture over the chicken. Set the remaining olive oil mixture aside. Seal the bag and massage to coat the chicken evenly. Refrigerate for 15 to 30 minutes.

Preheat a grill to medium-high or allow coals to burn down to white ash.

Drain the chicken and discard the marinade left in the bag. Grill the chicken for 5 to 6 minutes per side, or until golden brown and no longer pink inside and a meat thermometer inserted into the center registers 165°F. Place the chicken on a plate, cover with aluminum foil, and let rest for 5 minutes.

Toss together the lettuce, tomatoes, bell pepper, artichoke hearts, and onion in a salad bowl. Chop the chicken and add it to the salad. Whisk the Italian seasoning into the reserved olive oil mixture and drizzle it over the salad. Toss to coat. Sprinkle with Parmesan and serve.

TIPS:

» Salads are great to customize with the vegetables you enjoy and have on hand. For example, add ⅓ cup chopped cucumber, or substitute 1 chopped scallion for the red onion. If you enjoy olives, add ¼ cup chopped pitted ripe olives.

» Add 2 tablespoons minced fresh basil for a little spice or added flavor.

» Did you make the salad ahead? To ensure that the salad stays crisp and fresh, prepare the chopped salad but do not add the dressing. Cover and refrigerate the salad and dressing in separate containers. Toss together just before serving.

» Are there leftover marinated artichoke hearts in the jar? Cover and refrigerate for up to 5 days.

» Are you hearty eaters or just want extra chicken? If so, prepare and cook 2 chicken breasts as directed.

HERB-ROASTED CHICKEN
with ROSEMARY POTATOES

Nervous about those first few weeks of newlywed meals? This is a no-fail, knock-your-socks-off favorite with little prep required. Just pop the bird in the oven and let the golden skin develop. The aroma alone makes this a winner!

1 WHOLE CHICKEN, ABOUT 4
   POUNDS
8 TABLESPOONS (1 STICK)
   UNSALTED BUTTER, SOFTENED
2 LEMONS
3 SPRIGS FRESH ROSEMARY
¼ BUNCH FRESH THYME
3 TABLESPOONS MINCED FRESH
   FLAT-LEAF PARSLEY
KOSHER SALT AND FRESHLY
   GROUND BLACK PEPPER
½ TO 1 POUND NEW POTATOES,
   UNPEELED
1 TABLESPOON OLIVE OIL

SERVES 4

Preheat the oven to 400°F.

Pat the chicken dry with paper towels. Place the chicken breast side up in a large roasting pan (about 16¾ x 13¾ x 2½ inches).

Place the butter in a medium bowl. Zest the lemons onto the butter; reserve the lemons. Remove the leaves from 1 sprig of the rosemary and from 2 or 3 sprigs of the thyme and finely chop them. Add the chopped herbs and the parsley to the butter. Stir until the herbs and butter are well combined. Stir in salt and pepper to taste.

Use your hands to smear the butter all over the top, sides, and legs of the chicken. Cut the lemons in half and squeeze the juice from the lemons over the chicken.

Place the juiced lemon halves, 1 sprig of the rosemary, and the remaining thyme in the chicken cavity.

Place the potatoes in a zip-top bag. Remove the leaves from the remaining sprig of rosemary, finely chop them, and add to the potatoes. Drizzle the potatoes with the olive oil and massage to coat the potatoes evenly. Place the potatoes around the chicken.

Bake, uncovered, for 1 hour 15 minutes to 1 hour 30 minutes, or until the chicken is no longer pink inside and a meat thermometer inserted into the center of the breast or thigh registers 165°F. Baste the chicken with the drippings every 30 minutes.

Transfer the chicken to a platter, cover loosely with aluminum foil, and let rest for 10 minutes so that the juices have an opportunity to stay in the chicken. Using a slotted spoon, transfer the potatoes to a serving bowl. Carve the chicken and enjoy.

TIPS:

» You can use many combinations of fresh herbs for the chicken rub. Use your favorites!

» This recipe produces a traditional, French-style, crisp, juicy chicken. If you don't want to use butter, drizzle olive oil over the chicken and sprinkle with fresh herbs.

» Lemon halves are placed in the cavity, and yes, those are the same lemons you zested and juiced. There is still some flavor in those pieces, and they help make the chicken even tastier.

MISO-GINGER GLAZED SALMON

A miso-ginger glaze combines the classics of sweet and salty and complements the fish perfectly. This great dish is wonderful with a fresh salad and dinner is ready to serve in no time.

3 TABLESPOONS MIRIN

3 TABLESPOONS MISO, PREFERABLY YELLOW

1 TABLESPOON PACKED BROWN SUGAR

1 TABLESPOON REDUCED-SODIUM SOY SAUCE

2 TEASPOONS PEELED, MINCED FRESH GINGER

1½ TEASPOONS DARK SESAME OIL

1 TABLESPOON VEGETABLE OIL

2 SALMON FILLETS, 5 TO 6 OUNCES EACH

SERVES 2

Preheat the oven to 400°F.

Mix together the mirin, miso, brown sugar, soy sauce, ginger, and sesame oil in a small bowl. Set aside.

Heat the vegetable oil in a 10-inch cast-iron or other ovenproof skillet over medium heat. Add the salmon fillets, skin-side down, and cook for 5 minutes. Do not turn the salmon. Place the skillet in the oven and bake, uncovered, for 5 minutes.

Spoon the glaze over the fish. Return the skillet to the oven and bake, uncovered, for 3 to 4 minutes more, or until the fish is opaque and flakes easily with a fork.

To serve, spoon any glaze that may have collected in the skillet over the fish.

(continued)

TIPS:

» Miso is a paste made from fermented soybeans, salt, and usually some type of grain. It is salty and a little goes a long way, but it is rich in protein. Yellow miso is an all-purpose miso, while white miso is more delicate and red miso is more strongly flavored. Purchase miso at Asian markets or in the Asian foods section of larger grocery stores. Use a clean spoon to dip out the miso you need, then cover and refrigerate the remaining miso; it will keep for several months.

» Mirin is a sweet rice wine. At most grocery stores you will find small bottles stocked in the Asian foods section. If not available, you can substitute rice wine, dry sherry, or white wine in this recipe. As mirin is a sweet wine and the substitutes are not as sweet, you may want to stir an additional ½ to 1 teaspoon brown sugar into the glaze.

» If you have larger salmon fillets, maybe 10 to 12 ounces, cook just one fillet according the recipe, then cut it in half to serve.

» Ginger, in this recipe, is the knobby root that is readily available at most grocery stores. Do not use dry ground ginger. To prepare the fresh ginger, peel off the tough outer skin, but don't waste too much for the ginger just under the skin is very flavorful. One easy way to remove the skin is to scrape it off using the tip of a spoon. Once the skin is gone, grate the ginger needed for the recipe. If you have a larger piece of ginger than is needed, wrap it tightly and freeze it for up to 6 months. You can then slice off what you need and return the rest to the freezer.

POTATO & SALSA VERDE TORTILLAS

This is an excellent addition to your recipe arsenal, especially if you are implementing Meatless Mondays or want to incorporate more meatless fare into your weeknight meal plans.

½ POUND YUKON GOLD POTATOES (ABOUT 1 LARGE), UNPEELED, CUT INTO ½-INCH PIECES

1 TABLESPOON VEGETABLE OIL

½ MEDIUM ONION, SLICED THIN

2 CLOVES GARLIC, MINCED

⅓ CUP STORE-BOUGHT SALSA VERDE

¼ TEASPOON GROUND CUMIN

¼ TEASPOON DRIED OREGANO LEAVES

½ CUP DRAINED CANNED WHITE HOMINY

3 TABLESPOONS CRUMBLED QUESO FRESCO, PLUS MORE FOR SERVING

KOSHER SALT AND FRESHLY GROUND BLACK PEPPER

4 (6-INCH) FLOUR OR CORN TORTILLAS

SERVES 2

Place the potatoes in a 2- or 3-quart saucepan and add water to cover. Bring to a boil, reduce the heat, and simmer for 8 to 10 minutes, or until just tender (do not overcook). Drain well and set aside.

Meanwhile, heat the oil in a 10-inch nonstick skillet over medium heat. Add the onions and cook, stirring frequently, for about 10 minutes. Add the garlic and continue to cook for an additional minute. Stir in the salsa verde, cumin, oregano, and hominy. Add the cooked potatoes and the cheese. Season with salt and pepper to taste.

Heat an 8-inch nonstick skillet over medium-high heat. Place the tortillas, one at a time, in the skillet and cook to heat through, turning to heat both sides. Do not allow them to become crisp.

Divide the filling among the warm tortillas and sprinkle with additional cheese. Serve warm.

TIPS:

» Queso fresco cheese is similar to farmer's cheese in texture. It may also be labeled *queso blanco*. You can substitute feta cheese or shredded Monterey Jack cheese if you can't find it.

» Canned hominy is available in a white or yellow variety. You could substitute the yellow variety.

» Salsa verde is a green salsa that usually contains tomatillos, green chiles, and cilantro. This recipe works best with this green salsa.

CHIPOTLE CHICKEN TACOS

Why not pour a glass of sangria and deem tonight "Couple Cooking Night"? One of you can prepare the marinade while the other chops the vegetables. The canned chipotle pepper in adobo sauce catapults the flavor to cantina level in your own home. Keep canned chipotle peppers on hand in your pantry to add flavor and spice to many a meal (see Tips, page 22).

4 (6-INCH) FLOUR TORTILLAS

1½ TABLESPOONS CANOLA OIL,
     OLIVE OIL, OR VEGETABLE OIL

3 TABLESPOONS FRESH LIME JUICE

2 TEASPOONS FINELY CHOPPED
     GARLIC

1 TEASPOON GROUND CUMIN

1 TEASPOON CHILI POWDER

½ TEASPOON KOSHER SALT

1 TABLESPOON MINCED CHIPOTLE
     PEPPER IN ADOBO SAUCE

½ MEDIUM YELLOW ONION,
     THINLY SLICED

½ MEDIUM GREEN BELL PEPPER,
     CUT INTO THIN STRIPS

1½ CUPS SHREDDED COOKED
     CHICKEN (SEE TIPS, PAGE 70)

¼ CUP STORE-BOUGHT PICANTE
     SAUCE OR SALSA

¼ CUP SHREDDED LETTUCE

¼ CUP CRUMBLED QUESO FRESCO
     OR SHREDDED MONTEREY JACK
     CHEESE (SEE TIPS, PAGE 67)

SERVES 2

Preheat the oven to 200°F. Wrap the flour tortillas tightly in aluminum foil and place them in the oven to warm.

Whisk together the oil, lime juice, garlic, cumin, chili powder, salt, and minced chipotle pepper in a small bowl. Pour half of the marinade into a zip-top bag. Set aside the remainder.

Add the sliced onion and the bell pepper strips to the zip-top bag. Seal the bag, then massage to distribute the marinade evenly throughout.

Heat a 12-inch skillet over medium-high heat. Add the vegetables and cook, stirring frequently, for about 7 minutes, or until they are tender. Add the chicken and the reserved marinade, stir, and cook until heated through.

Divide the chicken mixture among the warm flour tortillas. Top with picante sauce, lettuce, and cheese.

(continued)

CHIPOTLE CHICKEN TACOS *(continued)*

1 TABLESPOON VEGETABLE OIL

2 BONELESS, SKINLESS CHICKEN
BREASTS, ABOUT 6 OUNCES
EACH

KOSHER SALT AND FRESHLY
GROUND BLACK PEPPER

¾ CUP REDUCED-SODIUM
CHICKEN BROTH OR WATER

SHREDDED CHICKEN (STOVETOP METHOD):

Heat the oil in a 12-inch nonstick skillet over medium-high heat. Pat the chicken dry with paper towels and season with salt and pepper on both sides. Place the chicken in the skillet and cook for 5 minutes, or until golden brown on one side. Turn the chicken and pour the broth into the skillet. Reduce the heat to maintain a simmer, cover, and simmer for 8 to 10 minutes, until the chicken is no longer pink inside and a meat thermometer inserted into the center registers 165°F. Remove the chicken from the skillet and allow it to cool. Shred the meat using two forks. The chicken can be prepared ahead and refrigerated for up to 3 days or frozen for up to 3 months.

3 TO 8 BONELESS SKINLESS
CHICKEN BREASTS, ABOUT
6 OUNCES EACH

KOSHER SALT AND FRESHLY
GROUND BLACK PEPPER

¾ CUP REDUCED-SODIUM
CHICKEN BROTH

SHREDDED CHICKEN (SLOW-COOKER METHOD):

Not only is this a great way to have chicken already cooked for these Chipotle Chicken Tacos, but you can also use the cooked chicken for casseroles or salads.

Spray a 4-quart slow cooker with nonstick spray. Season the chicken with salt and pepper and place them in the slow cooker. Add the broth. Cover and cook on low for 3 to 4 hours, or until the chicken is cooked through and very tender. Remove the chicken and allow it to cool, then shred the meat using two forks. Set aside the 1½ cups shredded chicken you need for this recipe, then divide the remaining shredded chicken into serving portions. Wrap, label, and freeze the chicken for up to 3 months. To defrost, place the frozen chicken in the refrigerator the night before you plan to use it.

TIPS:

» Use rotisserie chicken from the supermarket. Shred the meat using two forks.

» Other toppings might include sour cream or sliced avocado.

» See the chipotle pepper tip in the Pulled Pork Carnitas recipe on page 22.

PORK & POBLANO STREET TACOS

It may surprise you that you do not need to visit your local taqueria or food truck in order to enjoy street tacos that explode with flavor. Why not make this meal together? One of you can chop and prep garnishes and the other can sauté. Add a Mexican beer or a margarita and enjoy the experience.

1 LARGE POBLANO CHILE

½ POUND PORK TENDERLOIN

1½ TABLESPOONS VEGETABLE OIL

KOSHER SALT AND FRESHLY
    GROUND BLACK PEPPER

½ MEDIUM YELLOW ONION,
    CHOPPED

2 CLOVES GARLIC, MINCED

2 TABLESPOONS FRESH LIME JUICE

½ TEASPOON GROUND CUMIN

4 TO 6 (6-INCH) CORN OR FLOUR
    TORTILLAS, WARMED

CRUMBLED QUESO FRESCO OR
    OTHER MEXICAN CRUMBLED OR
    SHREDDED CHEESE (SEE TIPS,
    PAGE 67), FOR SERVING

COARSELY CHOPPED AVOCADO OR
    GUACAMOLE, FOR SERVING

STORE-BOUGHT SALSA VERDE,
    TOMATILLO SALSA, OR TOMATO
    SALSA,
    FOR SERVING

SERVES 2

Roast the poblano pepper over an open flame such as a grill, turning regularly until blistered or blackened all over, about 5 minutes, or place the pepper on a baking sheet and broil about 4 inches from the broiler element, turning frequently, for about 10 minutes. Place the charred pepper in a bowl and cover with plastic wrap. Set aside until cool enough to handle. Rub the blackened skin off the pepper, cut it in half, and rinse well to remove any remaining bits of skin and seeds. Dry well and chop.

Slice the pork tenderloin in half lengthwise. Thinly slice each half into thin strips.

Heat the oil in a 10-inch skillet over medium-high heat. Cook the pork in a single layer for 4 to 5 minutes, until browned on both sides. Season the pork with salt and pepper. Transfer the pork to a plate.

Add the onion to the skillet and cook, stirring frequently, until tender, about 5 minutes. Add the chopped poblano pepper and garlic. Cook, stirring continuously, for 1 to 2 minutes. Add the lime juice and cumin and stir well. Return the pork to the skillet and heat through.

Serve in warm tortillas. Garnish as desired with queso, avocado, and salsa.

TIPS:

» Our favorite with this recipe is lean pork tenderloin but you could substitute 1½ pounds boneless skinless chicken breasts for the pork.

WEEK
ENDS

ARTISAN CHEESE & WINE FONDUE
with ARTICHOKES & FRENCH BREAD

We prefer to use artisan cheese when possible, and can often find artisans or small, local dairies producing Fontina and Parmesan cheese. What is the difference between artisan cheese and that purchased under a national label? Artisan cheese refers to cheese produced in small batches by hand using the craftsmanship of skilled cheesemakers. It is often more complex in flavor. Of course, if artisan cheese is not available, feel free to substitute a similar cheese from the grocery store.

4 TABLESPOONS (½ STICK)
UNSALTED BUTTER

¼ CUP FINELY MINCED YELLOW
ONION

8 OUNCES BUTTON OR WILD
MUSHROOMS, THINLY SLICED

4 CLOVES GARLIC, MINCED

1 (12-OUNCE) JAR MARINATED
ARTICHOKE HEARTS, DRAINED
AND CHOPPED

½ CUP DRY WHITE WINE

4 OUNCES FONTINA CHEESE, CUT
INTO ½-INCH CUBES

8 OUNCES CREAM CHEESE, CUT
INTO ½-INCH CUBES

KOSHER SALT AND FRESHLY
GROUND BLACK PEPPER

¾ CUP SHREDDED PARMESAN
CHEESE

1 LOAF FRENCH BREAD, CUT INTO
PIECES FOR DIPPING

SERVES 4 TO 6

Melt the butter in a 12-inch nonstick skillet over medium-high heat. Add the onion and mushrooms and cook, stirring frequently, for 8 to 10 minutes, or until the mushrooms are tender and their liquid has evaporated. Stir in the garlic and cook for 30 seconds more.

Add the artichoke hearts and wine to the mixture. Bring to a simmer, reduce the heat as needed to maintain a simmer, and cook for 5 to 10 minutes. Add the Fontina, cream cheese, and salt and pepper to taste. Stir until the cheese has melted and the mixture is smooth. Add the Parmesan and cook, stirring, until melted.

Pour the mixture into a fondue pot and keep warm. Serve with French bread.

(continued)

TIPS:

» This is excellent served with fresh vegetables such as broccoli and cauliflower.

» For artichoke and spinach fondue: Omit the mushrooms and substitute 1½ cups fresh trimmed spinach leaves, coarsely chopped. Add the spinach to the onions, cook 2 to 3 minutes, then proceed as recipe directs.

» Fondue pots are available in electric and nonelectric versions. Those that are not electric generally keep the fondue warm by holding it over a can of burning Sterno. Be sure to keep an extra can of Sterno in the pantry so you do not run out. If using an electric fondue pot, follow the manufacturer's directions for the best temperature, but generally a cheese fondue needs a low temperature. If you do not have a fondue pot, you can keep this fondue warm in a small slow cooker.

» Freshly grated Parmesan cheese adds more flavor than packaged shredded Parmesan cheese. To grate the Parmesan cheese, use a rasp-style grater, such as a Microplane. To "grate" this hard cheese in a food processor, allow the Parmesan to come to room temperature, cut it into 1-inch cubes, and place them in the work bowl of the food processor fitted with the metal chopping blade; pulse to very finely chop.

GARLIC SHRIMP RISOTTO

Yes, it takes time, and one of you needs to stir continuously for about 20 minutes, but Garlic Shrimp Risotto is a comforting dish to make on a cold night. Take turns stirring, pour a glass of wine, and look at this as the ideal time to talk to each other. The rewards, both in terms of your dinner and conversation time with your honey, are worth the effort.

3½ CUPS LOW-SODIUM CHICKEN
    BROTH
2 TABLESPOONS UNSALTED
    BUTTER
1 SHALLOT, MINCED
2 CLOVES GARLIC, MINCED
1 CUP UNCOOKED ARBORIO RICE
KOSHER SALT AND FRESHLY
    GROUND BLACK PEPPER
¼ CUP DRY WHITE WINE
6 TO 8 OUNCES FRESH SHELLED
    AND DEVEINED SHRIMP, OR
    FROZEN SHRIMP, SHELLED,
    THAWED, AND DRAINED
½ CUP FROZEN PEAS, THAWED
½ CUP SHREDDED PARMESAN
    CHEESE
1 TABLESPOON MINCED FRESH
    FLAT-LEAF PARSLEY

SERVES 4

Heat the chicken broth in a 2-quart saucepan over medium heat until steaming hot. Reduce the heat to very low, cover, and keep the broth warm.

Melt the butter in a 4-quart saucepan over medium heat. Stir in the shallot and cook, stirring frequently, for 2 minutes. Stir in the garlic and cook, stirring frequently, for 30 seconds. Stir in the rice and cook, stirring frequently, until the rice begins to turn golden, about 3 minutes. Stir in the salt and pepper to taste and the wine and cook, stirring continuously, until the rice has absorbed the wine.

Set a timer for 20 minutes. Stir about ½ cup of the hot broth into the risotto. Cook, stirring continuously, until the rice has absorbed all of the broth. Continue to add hot broth in ½-cup increments, stirring until the rice has absorbed the broth after each addition. (Cooking the rice and adding all of the broth should take about 20 minutes. Generally, add broth to the rice every 2 to 3 minutes.)

Just after stirring in the last of the broth, stir in the shrimp and peas. Cook, stirring continuously, for 2 to 3 minutes, or until the shrimp begin to turn pink. Stir in the Parmesan.

Remove from the heat, spoon into a serving bowl, and garnish with the parsley.

(continued)

TIPS:

» The exact amount of liquid the rice will absorb may vary a little. If, after you have stirred in the last of the hot broth, you wish to make the risotto a little more moist, heat an additional ½ cup broth until steaming hot and gradually stir it into the cooked risotto. This tip works well for risotto cooked on the stove or in a slow cooker.

» What is arborio rice? This is a short-grained Italian rice, and since the short grains become moist and stick together as they cook, it is used to achieve the classic creamy texture desired for risotto.

» What is a shallot? A shallot is a member of the onion family, but it is known for its mild flavor that has hints of both garlic and onion. In appearance, it may remind you of a large garlic clove for the head has multiple cloves (often two of them), with each clove covered with papery skin. As this recipe lists one shallot, use just one of the cloves of the shallot, peel away the papery skin and mince it finely.

» To prepare the risotto in a slow cooker, spray a 4-quart slow cooker with nonstick spray. Melt the butter in a 4-quart saucepan and cook the shallot, garlic, and rice as directed above, then pour it into the slow cooker. Return the pan to the heat and add 2½ cups of the chicken broth. Heat until the broth comes to a boil. Pour the boiling broth into the rice in the slow cooker and stir well. Cover and cook on high for 2 hours, stirring after 1 hour.

Pour the remaining 1 cup broth into a small microwave-safe glass bowl or measuring cup. Microwave on high for 3 minutes or until it boils. Gradually stir the boiling broth into the rice in the slow cooker, stirring continuously. Stir in the shrimp and peas. Cover and cook on high for 10 to 15 minutes, or until the shrimp are tender and turn pink. Stir in the Parmesan cheese. Sprinkle with the parsley.

VEGETARIAN LASAGNA

What an exceptional recipe to "sneak" vegetables into the menu and it is guaranteed that non-veggie lovers will devour this with abandon. This can be made ahead for easy entertaining.

2 TABLESPOONS OLIVE OIL

1 LARGE ONION, CHOPPED

1 LARGE FENNEL BULB, CHOPPED

3 MEDIUM CARROTS, CHOPPED

1 (12-OUNCE) JAR MARINATED
    ARTICHOKE HEARTS, DRAINED
    AND CHOPPED

3 CLOVES GARLIC, MINCED

3 CUPS MARINARA SAUCE
    (PAGE 28) OR 1 (23-OUNCE)
    JAR MARINARA SAUCE

12 TO 14 LASAGNA NOODLES
    (ABOUT 12 OUNCES)

1 LARGE EGG, LIGHTLY BEATEN

1 (15-OUNCE) CONTAINER LOW-
    FAT RICOTTA CHEESE

3 CUPS SHREDDED MOZZARELLA
    CHEESE

½ CUP SHREDDED PARMESAN
    CHEESE

1½ CUPS FRESH TRIMMED
    SPINACH LEAVES, COARSELY
    CHOPPED

SERVES 8

Heat the olive oil in a Dutch oven over medium high heat. Add the onion, fennel, carrots, artichoke hearts, and garlic and cook, stirring frequently, for 3 to 4 minutes, or until the vegetables are crisp-tender. Stir in the marinara. Reduce the heat and simmer, covered, for 15 to 20 minutes.

Cook the lasagna according to the package directions. Drain.

Preheat the oven to 350°F. Spray a 9 x 13-inch pan with nonstick spray. Combine the egg, ricotta, 2 cups mozzarella, ¼ cup Parmesan, and spinach.

Spoon 1 cup of the sauce into the pan and spread to coat evenly. Arrange 4 lasagna noodles lengthwise over the sauce. Spoon ½ of the ricotta mixture evenly over the noodles. Top with 1 cup of the sauce.

Arrange 4 lasagna noodles crosswise over the sauce, cutting to fit as necessary. Spoon the remaining ricotta mixture evenly over the noodles. Top with 1 cup of the sauce.

Arrange 4 lasagna noodles lengthwise over the sauce. Spoon the remaining sauce over the noodles. Cover with aluminum foil. Bake for 30 minutes. Uncover. Top with the remaining 1 cup mozzarella and remaining ¼ cup Parmesan. Bake uncovered for 15 minutes, or until hot and bubbly.

TIPS:

» To freeze: Assemble and bake, omitting the cheese topping. Refrigerate until cool, then wrap, label, and freeze. Remove from the freezer before serving, so it partially thaws. Bake at 350°F about 30 to 40 minutes or until heated through. Add cheese and bake for 15 minutes.

WINTER CHICKEN, ARTICHOKE & FENNEL CASSOULET

Winter Chicken, Artichoke, and Fennel Cassoulet really is a perfect dinner on a cold night. The fennel, sun-dried tomatoes, and artichokes create a modern flair, but the beans and chicken mean the dish offers classic, comforting flavors.

1 TABLESPOON VEGETABLE OIL

2 BONE-IN, SKIN-ON CHICKEN
BREAST HALVES (SEE TIPS,
PAGE 82)

KOSHER SALT AND FRESHLY
GROUND BLACK PEPPER

1 MEDIUM FENNEL BULB, TRIMMED
AND QUARTERED

½ MEDIUM SWEET YELLOW
ONION, QUARTERED

2 CLOVES GARLIC, MINCED

1 CUP REDUCED-SODIUM CHICKEN
BROTH

⅓ CUP CHOPPED SUN-DRIED
TOMATOES IN OIL, DRAINED

1 TEASPOON ITALIAN SEASONING

¼ TEASPOON RED PEPPER FLAKES

1 (14-OUNCE) CAN QUARTERED
ARTICHOKE HEARTS, DRAINED

1 (16-OUNCE) CAN GREAT
NORTHERN BEANS, RINSED AND
DRAINED

2 TABLESPOONS MINCED FRESH
FLAT-LEAF PARSLEY OR MINCED
FENNEL FRONDS, FOR SERVING

SERVES 2 TO 4

Preheat the oven to 375°F.

Heat the oil in a 12-inch ovenproof skillet with a lid over medium-high heat. Add the chicken, skin-side down, and cook for 5 minutes, or until well browned. Turn and cook for 3 to 4 minutes more, or until well browned. Season with salt and pepper. Transfer the chicken to a plate.

Add the fennel and onion to the skillet and cook, stirring frequently, for 3 minutes, or until the onion is tender. Stir in the garlic and cook for 30 seconds. Stir in the chicken broth, sun-dried tomatoes, Italian seasoning, and red pepper flakes. Heat until the liquid boils, then reduce the heat to maintain a simmer and cook for 1 minute. Return the chicken breasts to the skillet, skin-side up. Pour the artichoke hearts and beans over the chicken.

Cover and bake for 30 minutes, or until the chicken is no longer pink inside and a meat thermometer inserted in the center registers 165°F. Remove from the oven and let rest, covered, for 5 minutes. Sprinkle with the parsley.

(continued)

TIPS:

» Chicken breasts sold today are often quite large—and bone-in halves can each weigh up to 1 pound. If the chicken pieces are large, you may find one piece is the perfect amount to share—especially since there are lots of vegetables in this hearty dish. This dish reheats wonderfully so leftovers may be welcome!

» Pat the chicken dry with a paper towel before cooking to ensure better, more even browning.

» Bone-in pieces of chicken add to the flavor in the dish. If you wish to use boneless skinless chicken breasts, you may do so. Cook as directed, but reduce the roasting time to about 20 minutes or until the chicken is no longer pink inside and a meat thermometer inserted in the center registers 165°F.

» Have you ever cooked fennel? This flavorful plant has stems that look somewhat like celery, fronds that can serve as an herb, and a bulbous end that is cooked and served as a vegetable. For this dish, cut off the stems and leaves to mince for the garnish or to use in another dish, and use just the bulb end. Trim away any tough or dry outer leaves from the bulb, then cut the bulb into quarters.

» If desired, or if an ovenproof skillet is not available, brown the chicken as directed in a skillet, then place it in a 2½- to 3-quart casserole. Cook the vegetables in the skillet as directed, add the broth and seasonings, and bring to a boil. Spoon the vegetables over the chicken and pour the broth over all. Cover and bake as directed.

MUSHROOMS & CARAMELIZED ONION EGG SKILLET

You can spend a lazy weekend morning at home together and enjoy this fantastic Mushroom and Caramelized Onion Egg Skillet for a late breakfast or brunch. It will remind you of a favorite dish at the neighborhood breakfast spot, but you won't have to get dressed up to go out and enjoy it.

2 TABLESPOONS UNSALTED
  BUTTER

½ MEDIUM SWEET YELLOW
  ONION, HALVED AND THINLY
  SLICED

1 CUP SLICED BUTTON OR WILD
  MUSHROOMS

½ TEASPOON DRIED THYME
  LEAVES

KOSHER SALT AND FRESHLY
  GROUND BLACK PEPPER

4 LARGE EGGS

¼ CUP MILK

¼ CUP CHOPPED JARRED ROASTED
  RED PEPPERS, DRAINED

½ CUP SHREDDED SWISS CHEESE

½ CUP TRIMMED SPINACH OR
  KALE LEAVES, TORN INTO
  PIECES (OPTIONAL)

SERVES 2

Melt the butter in a 10-inch nonstick skillet over medium heat. Add the onion and cook, uncovered, stirring frequently, for 10 to 12 minutes, or until the onions begin to caramelize. Add the mushrooms and season with the thyme and salt and black pepper to taste. Cook, stirring frequently, for 5 minutes, or until the onions are a deep golden color, the mushrooms are tender, and the liquid has evaporated. Spoon into a bowl and set aside.

Whisk together the eggs and milk in a small bowl. Season with salt and black pepper. Return the skillet to the stovetop over low heat. Pour the egg mixture into the skillet and cook, stirring frequently but gently, until the eggs are almost set. Stir in the roasted red pepper. Stir in the cheese and onion-mushroom mixture and cook, stirring gently, until the eggs are set. If desired, stir in the spinach and cook just until wilted.

TIPS:

» Do you wonder what kind of mushrooms to use? Wild mushrooms, such as shiitake or morel mushrooms, are more flavorful and provide a deeper, earthy accent. Button mushrooms are more readily available. Use a combination of mushrooms or the variety that you prefer.

OVEN-TOASTED HAM & EGG TARTINE SANDWICHES

A tartine is an open-faced French sandwich. Imagine that you two are strolling the romantic streets of Paris and can stop at one of the little cafés that dot the streets. Don't forget to linger over the café au lait! What a great way to start your morning.

2 SLICES CRUSTY WHOLE-GRAIN
    BREAD OR COUNTRY WHITE
    BREAD, TOASTED

2 TABLESPOONS PLUS 1 TEASPOON
    UNSALTED BUTTER

2 THIN SLICES COOKED HAM

2 SLICES GRUYÈRE OR SWISS
    CHEESE

2 LARGE EGGS

KOSHER SALT AND FRESHLY
    GROUND BLACK PEPPER

SERVES 2

Preheat the oven to 400°F.

Lightly spread one side of each piece of toast with about ½ teaspoon of the butter. Place the toast, buttered-side up, in a single layer in an 11 x 7-inch baking dish or on a 10 x 15-inch baking sheet.

Top each slice of toast with a slice of ham and then a slice of cheese. Bake, uncovered, for 5 minutes, or until hot and the cheese has melted.

Meanwhile, melt the remaining 2 tablespoons butter in an 8-inch nonstick skillet over medium heat. Break one egg into a custard cup, then slip the egg into the butter. Repeat with the second egg. Season the eggs with salt and pepper. Cook until the egg whites set.

Carefully turn the eggs and cook on the second side until the egg yolk is done as desired. (As an alternative, to serve the eggs sunny-side up, using the tip of a small spoon, baste the egg yolks with melted butter. Cover and cook for 1 minute. Continue to baste the egg yolk, then cover and cook until the egg yolks are thickened and done as desired.)

Place the cooked eggs on top of the ham and cheese on the toast and serve immediately.

(continued)

TIPS:

» Use thin slices of deli ham or leftover ham. Sliced Black Forest or Virginia ham will have more flavor than deli-shaved ham, and slices of country ham will be packed with a distinctive flavor. Of course, use the ham that you prefer and that is available. To boost the flavor if using a milder-flavored ham, toast the bread as directed, then lightly spread each slice with Dijon mustard and top with ham and cheese.

» Breaking the eggs into a custard cup, then gently slipping them into the hot skillet will make a more attractive egg.

» Cook eggs until the egg yolk thickens—it need not be firm. The very young, the elderly, pregnant women, and those who are ill or who have weakened immune systems should avoid eating uncooked or undercooked eggs.

» Does your small skillet have a lid? Check to see if a lid for one of your saucepans fits the skillet. Frequently, the pot and pan manufacturers sell "open stock" covers that will fit your skillet perfectly. Housewares and kitchen shops also sell lids in a variety of sizes, or in a pinch, you can use the bottom of a baking sheet. Flexible silicone lids for bowls are now readily available. Read the label on these lids carefully as some are safe to use when cooking and others are only safe for reheating in the microwave but are not safe to use on a pan on the stove. Be sure to check with the manufacturer if you are not sure—and do not take chances.

BRIOCHE FRENCH TOAST

Lazy-dazey weekend mornings call for a make-ahead breakfast. Pull the covers back over your head and know that a memorable meal is minutes away.

3 (1½-INCH) SLICES BRIOCHE LOAF

3 LARGE EGGS

1 CUP HALF-AND-HALF

2 TEASPOONS PURE VANILLA
   EXTRACT

½ TEASPOON GROUND
   CINNAMON

8 TABLESPOONS (1 STICK)
   UNSALTED BUTTER

⅓ CUP PACKED BROWN SUGAR

¼ CUP MAPLE SYRUP

1 TABLESPOON BOURBON

PINCH OF TABLE SALT

½ CUP COARSELY CHOPPED
   PECANS, TOASTED

SERVES 4 TO 6

Spray a 7 x 11-inch baking dish with nonstick spray. Cut each bread slice in half. Arrange the bread slices in a single layer in the prepared dish.

Whisk together the eggs, half-and-half, vanilla, and cinnamon in a small bowl. Pour the egg mixture over the brioche slices. Cover with plastic wrap and refrigerate for at least 3 hours or overnight.

Preheat the oven to 350°F.

Remove the brioche from the refrigerator. Heat the butter, brown sugar, maple syrup, bourbon, and salt in a 1-quart saucepan over medium heat, stirring frequently, until the butter has melted and the mixture begins to bubble and foam. Pour the butter sauce over the bread slices. Bake, uncovered, for 35 to 40 minutes or until golden. Remove from the oven and baste with the sauce from the dish. Sprinkle the pecans evenly over brioche. Serve warm.

TIPS:

» If desired, omit the bourbon.

» Substitute 1½-inch-thick slices of French bread for the brioche. Cut enough slices to cover the bottom of the baking dish. Proceed as directed.

» Toasting pecans intensifies their flavor. To toast the pecans, spread them in a single layer on a baking sheet. Toast in a preheated 350°F oven for 5 to 7 minutes, or until lightly toasted.

GOAT CHEESE AUX FINES HERBES OMELET

What sounds good for that leisurely breakfast? Or, maybe you spent the day together, out at flea markets, antiques shops, or art galleries, searching for a special little accent piece, so a simple dinner at home sounds too good to pass up. Either way, goat cheese and fresh herbs boost the flavor of an omelet to lofty heights.

1 TO 2 SPRIGS FRESH FLAT-LEAF
  PARSLEY, FINELY MINCED

1 TO 2 SPRIGS FRESH TARRAGON,
  FINELY MINCED

2 FRESH CHIVES, FINELY MINCED

4 LARGE EGGS

KOSHER SALT AND FRESHLY
  GROUND BLACK PEPPER

1 TABLESPOON UNSALTED BUTTER

¼ CUP GOAT CHEESE CRUMBLES

SERVES 2

Combine the minced herbs in a small bowl. Set aside.

Whisk together 2 of the eggs, 1 tablespoon water, and salt and pepper in a small bowl.

Melt half of the butter in an 8-inch nonstick skillet over medium-low heat. Pour the egg mixture into the skillet. Cook gently until the bottom is set. Using the edge of a spatula or pancake turner, gently lift the edge of the cooked eggs away from the skillet, then tilt the pan slightly to allow the uncooked eggs to flow around the edges and under the omelet. Repeat, gently lifting the edges and tilting the pan until most of the eggs are cooked and the top is softly set.

Sprinkle about half of the herbs and half of the goat cheese over half of the omelet. Gently fold the omelet over the herbs and cheese. Transfer to a plate and keep warm.

Repeat with remaining ingredients to make a second omelet.

TIPS:

» Fines herbes is a classic French herb mixture and traditionally includes chives, tarragon, and parsley or chervil. Chervil is more difficult to find, so in this case, fresh parsley is used.

» How do you mince fresh herbs? Herbs that are dry will mince more easily, so rinse and pat them dry with paper towels. Remove and discard tough stems. Place the herbs on a cutting board. Hold the tip of a large chef's knife down with one hand and use a rocking motion to cut through the stack of herbs. Gather the leaves together again into a pile and repeat until the herbs are as finely minced as you wish. An alternate way is to drop the herbs into a small, deep bowl or cup and mince using the tips of kitchen shears.

» You can follow these basic directions to make any flavor of omelet you can imagine. Top the cooked eggs with other minced herbs or other cheeses. If you top an omelet with vegetables or meats, cook the vegetables or meat until they are tender or cooked through before topping the omelet.

BLT DEVILED EGGS

These are not your mother's deviled eggs. The addition of bacon, lettuce, and tomato launch these eggs into today's food arena. They are perfect for picnics, pretheater fare, and late-night noshing.

4 LARGE EGGS, HARD-BOILED
AND PEELED

2 TABLESPOONS LIGHT
MAYONNAISE

1 TEASPOON PREPARED MUSTARD

SEVERAL DASHES OF HOT SAUCE

2 SLICES BACON, COOKED UNTIL
CRISP THEN CRUMBLED

2 CHERRY TOMATOES, SEEDED
AND FINELY CHOPPED

KOSHER SALT AND FRESHLY
GROUND BLACK PEPPER

2 TABLESPOONS FINELY SHREDDED
LETTUCE

SERVES 2 TO 4

Slice the eggs in half lengthwise. Remove the yolks and place them in a medium bowl; set the whites aside. Mash the yolks and stir in the mayonnaise, mustard, and hot sauce. Gently fold in three quarters of the bacon and the cherry tomatoes. Add salt and pepper to taste.

Fill the egg white halves evenly with the yolk mixture and garnish with lettuce. Sprinkle evenly with the remaining crumbled bacon.

Serve immediately or store, covered, in the refrigerator until ready to serve.

TIPS:

» For Jalapeño Deviled Eggs, prepare as directed above, omitting the lettuce and garnishing with 2 tablespoons finely chopped, drained, pickled jalapeños.

» What is the best way to hard-boil an egg? The name of these eggs is really "hard-cooked" because for the best results you really do not boil the eggs. Place the eggs in a single layer in a saucepan and add cold water to cover the eggs by a depth of 1 inch. Heat until the water just begins to boil. Remove the pan from the heat, cover it, and allow the eggs to stand in the hot water for about 12 minutes. Drain and cool under cold running water, then peel.

» To pack for a picnic, make the BLT Deviled Eggs as directed and refrigerate in a sealed container. Pack the container in a cooler along with a frozen ice or gel pack.

CHICKEN & SWISS POP TARTS

These savory chicken and cheese tarts are perfect to take on a picnic. The tasty chicken filling is neatly sealed inside the buttery pastry, making them easy to pack, serve, and eat. They are small, so be sure to pack plenty.

CRUST:

1¼ CUPS ALL-PURPOSE FLOUR

2 TABLESPOONS SHREDDED PARMESAN CHEESE

½ TEASPOON TABLE SALT

4 TABLESPOONS (½ STICK) COLD UNSALTED BUTTER, CUT INTO 4 PIECES

¼ CUP VEGETABLE SHORTENING

1 LARGE EGG, SEPARATED

2 TO 2½ TABLESPOONS COLD MILK

FILLING:

½ CUP FINELY CHOPPED COOKED CHICKEN

¼ CUP SHREDDED SWISS CHEESE

2 TABLESPOONS GARDEN VEGETABLE–FLAVORED WHIPPED CREAM CHEESE SPREAD

2 TABLESPOONS CHOPPED JARRED ROASTED RED PEPPERS, DRAINED

⅛ TEASPOON GARLIC POWDER

KOSHER SALT AND FRESHLY GROUND BLACK PEPPER

MAKES 6 TARTS

MAKE THE CRUST: Whisk together the flour, Parmesan, and salt in a bowl. Using a pastry cutter or two knives, cut in the butter and vegetable shortening until the mixture resembles coarse even crumbs. Stir together the egg yolk and 2 tablespoons of the milk. Add the egg-milk mixture to the flour mixture. Using a fork, lightly stir until the flour is moistened. If additional moisture is needed, add the remaining ½ tablespoon milk, 1 teaspoon at a time, until the flour is moistened. Gather the dough into a ball. Divide the dough in half; wrap each portion in plastic wrap and refrigerate for several hours or overnight.

MAKE THE FILLING: Stir together all the ingredients in a small bowl until combined.

ASSEMBLE THE TARTS: Preheat the oven to 350°F. Line a baking sheet with parchment paper.

Roll each piece of dough into a 6 x 12-inch rectangle on a floured board. Cut each into 6 (3 x 4-inch) rectangles, making a total of 12 rectangles. Place 6 of the rectangles on the prepared baking sheet, about 1 inch apart.

Evenly divide the filling among 6 of the pastry rectangles, spooning about 1½ to 2 tablespoons of filling into the center of each pastry. Spread lightly, leaving a ½-inch border.

Whisk together the egg white and 1 tablespoon cold water in a small bowl. Brush the border of each pastry rectangle lightly with the egg white mixture. Place a second rectangle of dough directly over the first. Use the tines of a fork to seal the edges of the pastry together. Prick the top pastry several times with a fork. Brush the top lightly with the egg white mixture. Bake for 23 to 26 minutes, or until golden. Transfer the tarts to a wire rack to cool.

TIPS:

» To make the dough for the crust in a food processor, place the flour, Parmesan, and salt in the work bowl of a food processor and pulse to blend. Add the butter and vegetable shortening and pulse until both are evenly cut into the flour mixture. Add the egg yolk and 2 tablespoons milk to the work bowl. Process just until the mixture comes together and forms a ball. Proceed as directed.

» Substitute 1 (4.5-ounce) can chunk chicken breast, drained and flaked, for the ½ cup chopped cooked chicken.

» These tarts are just as good served chilled at a picnic. To pack for a picnic, make the Chicken and Swiss Pop Tarts the day before and cool completely. Pack the tarts between layers of paper towel and place in a zip-top bag. Place the sealed bag of tarts in the refrigerator overnight. Pack the bag in a cooler along with a frozen ice or gel pack.

» Do you know how to separate an egg? The best way is to use an egg separa-tor—readily available where kitchen utensils and gadgets are sold. If you don't have one, pour the egg through your clean fingers, allowing the white to drip into a small bowl and cupping the yolk in your palm. Pouring the yolk back and forth between eggshell halves is no longer recommended as the shells can harbor bacteria.

GRAZING &
SMALL PLATES

APRICOT-ALMOND BAKED BRIE

Apricot-Almond Baked Brie is elegant to serve and takes just moments to prepare. Even better, you can make it early in the day, refrigerate, and then bake it just before your guests come. What a treat!

¼ CUP CHOPPED DRIED APRICOTS

½ CUP BOILING WATER

¼ CUP APRICOT PRESERVES

¼ TEASPOON PURE ALMOND
EXTRACT

1 SHEET PUFF PASTRY, THAWED (½
OF A 17.3-OUNCE PACKAGE)

2 TABLESPOONS SLICED ALMONDS,
TOASTED

1 (8-OUNCE) BRIE CHEESE ROUND

1 LARGE EGG

1 TABLESPOON COLD WATER

WATER CRACKERS OR YOUR
FAVORITE CRACKERS, FOR
SERVING

SERVES 6

Preheat the oven to 400°F. Line a baking sheet with parchment paper.

Combine the dried apricots and boiling water in a 2-cup glass measuring cup. Let stand for 15 minutes. Drain and discard the water. Stir the apricot preserves and almond extract into the apricots. Set aside.

Unfold the puff pastry sheet on a lightly floured board. Roll to flatten it slightly. Use the tip of a knife to trim off the corners so the sheet is a slightly more rounded shape.

Spoon the almonds into the center of the pastry, loosely sprinkling them into a circle about 4 inches in diameter, or roughly the size of the Brie. Spoon the apricot mixture over the almonds, again roughly estimating the diameter of the Brie. Gently place the Brie on top of the apricot mixture.

Beat the egg with the cold water. Brush the outer edge of the pastry with the egg-water wash. Bring the edges of the pastry up and pinch together tightly, sealing the Brie and the apricots in a pastry envelope. Turn the packet over and place the Brie, seam-side down, on the lined baking sheet. If desired, use the corners trimmed off the pastry to make decorations and use the egg-water wash to "glue" the decorations to the top of the Brie (see Tips, page 97).

Bake for 20 to 25 minutes, or until the pastry is golden brown. Let stand for 5 to 10 minutes before serving. Serve warm with crackers.

TIPS:

» To decorate the Brie, you might find inspiration from the seasons or holidays. For example, gather up the scraps and roll them into a long strip. Shape the strip into a loose bow and center it on top of the Brie, using the egg-water wash as "glue." Or roll the scraps flat and use cookie cutters to cut out holly leaves, stars, hearts, or flowers. "Glue" the cut pastry shapes on the top-center of the Brie.

» Can you eat the rind on Brie? Sure, and many feel it is the best part. There is no need to trim the rind off the Brie before you wrap it in the pastry or while enjoying it.

» Toasting the almonds intensifies their flavor. To toast the almonds, spread the almonds in a single layer on a baking sheet. Toast in a preheated 350°F oven for 5 to 7 minutes, or until golden.

CROSTINI *with* GARLIC CONFIT, TOMATOES & PARMESAN

Confit historically referred to preserved meat, but today we have used the idea same to poach garlic in oil. The cloves will be soft and buttery and the flavor mild yet sweet. These fantastic crostini feature the garlic confit and are topped with roasted cherry tomatoes for a winning combination.

GARLIC CONFIT:

¼ CUP GARLIC CLOVES, PEELED
(ABOUT 15 GARLIC CLOVES)
½ CUP OLIVE OIL

ROASTED TOMATOES:

1 CUP CHERRY TOMATOES, HALVED
KOSHER SALT AND FRESHLY
GROUND BLACK PEPPER
2 TEASPOONS BALSAMIC VINEGAR

TO ASSEMBLE:

14 TO 16 SLICES FRENCH
BAGUETTE
2 TABLESPOONS MINCED FRESH
BASIL, PLUS MORE FOR SERVING
¼ CUP SHREDDED PARMESAN
CHEESE, OR THIN SLICES OF
PARMESAN CHEESE

MAKES 14 TO 16 CROSTINI

MAKE THE GARLIC CONFIT: In a 1-quart saucepan, combine the garlic cloves and olive oil. Heat over low heat until the oil is just hot and small bubbles begin to appear. Reduce the heat to very low and cook, uncovered, for 40 to 45 minutes, or until the garlic cloves are very tender. (The garlic should not brown.) Remove from the heat and allow to cool completely.

Drain the garlic, reserving the olive oil, and place the garlic in a small bowl. Using a fork, mash the garlic until nearly smooth.

MAKE THE ROASTED TOMATOES: Preheat the oven to 400°F. Line a 10 x 15-inch jelly-roll pan or rimmed baking sheet with aluminum foil.

Place the cherry tomatoes in a zip-top bag. Drizzle with 1 tablespoon of the reserved olive oil and season with salt and pepper. Seal the bag and massage gently to coat the tomatoes evenly. Pour the tomatoes into a single layer in the prepared pan. Bake for 15 minutes, stirring midway through. Remove from the oven. Drizzle with the balsamic vinegar and toss gently to coat. Set aside to cool.

ASSEMBLE THE DISH: When ready to serve, toast the French bread slices under the broiler until golden brown. Allow to cool until you are able to handle the toast. Spread a light coating of the garlic paste on one side of each slice of toasted bread.

Stir the 2 tablespoons basil into the tomatoes. Divide the tomatoes evenly among the crostini. Garnish with Parmesan and additional minced basil.

(continued)

TIPS:

» When making the garlic confit, make a shallow layer of garlic in a small sauce-pan, and pour in enough olive oil to cover the garlic. If a garlic clove is especially large, cut it in half so that it is submerged in the olive oil and cooks more evenly. If ½ cup olive oil does not cover all of the garlic, add additional olive oil until it generously covers all of the garlic. Cook until the garlic is very tender, but watch the process and keep the heat very low so the garlic does not brown.

» Garlic confit is a wonderful treat to make and keep refrigerated to use when needed, so if desired, increase the garlic to ½ cup and cover with about ¾ cup olive oil. Cook as directed, then spoon out about half of the garlic to use in this recipe. Place the remaining garlic in a small jar and pour the reserved olive oil over the garlic, taking care to submerge the garlic completely. Cover and store in the refrigerator for up to 1 week.

Use a clean spoon to lift out the garlic confit or the seasoned oil to avoid cross-contamination. Add garlic confit to mashed potatoes for an instant flavor boost, use it to season roast chicken, or to flavor pizza or sandwiches, or spread it on focaccia or flatbread. The garlic-flavored oil is wonderful as a base for a vinaigrette, to brush over chicken for grilling, or to season vegetables when roasting. Use either the garlic confit or the garlic-flavored oil within 1 week.

» For make-ahead convenience, make the garlic confit early in the day or the day before and refrigerate it overnight.

FLATBREAD *with* ROASTED ASPARAGUS & FONTINA

Flatbread ingredients can be altered to match what you have on hand, so feel free to change the vegetables or add meat. The perk with this recipe is that it can be made on one of those nights when you truly have no idea what's for dinner and you cannot imagine spending a lot of time in the kitchen.

2 TABLESPOONS OLIVE OIL

2 CLOVES GARLIC, MINCED

8 OUNCES FRESH ASPARAGUS

KOSHER SALT AND FRESHLY
   GROUND BLACK PEPPER

1 TABLESPOON UNSALTED BUTTER

4 OUNCES BUTTON OR WILD
   MUSHROOMS, THINLY SLICED

2 NAAN OR PITA BREADS

2/3 CUP SHREDDED FONTINA
   CHEESE

SERVES 2 TO 4

Preheat the oven to 450°F.

Combine the olive oil and garlic in a small bowl. Pour half of the olive oil mixture into a gallon-size zip-top bag.

Snap off the woody ends of the asparagus, and if desired, remove the scales. Place the asparagus in the bag, seal the bag, and massage gently to distribute the oil and garlic evenly.

Place the asparagus in a single layer on a rimmed baking sheet. Season with salt and pepper. Roast, uncovered, for 5 to 7 minutes, or until the asparagus is tender. Set aside until cool enough to handle, then cut the asparagus into 1½-inch pieces.

Meanwhile, melt the butter in a 6-inch nonstick skillet over medium-high heat. Add the mushrooms and cook, stirring frequently, for 5 to 6 minutes, until the mushrooms are cooked and their liquid has evaporated.

Place the naan on a rimmed baking sheet and brush evenly with the remaining olive oil–garlic mixture. Sprinkle the asparagus and mushrooms evenly over the bread. Sprinkle evenly with Fontina. Bake for 8 to 10 minutes, or until the cheese has melted and the crust is crisp.

Cut into slices and serve.

(continued)

TIPS:

» How large is the naan you are using? You may find that one naan, topped with half of the other ingredients, is plenty for you two. Others may wish to cook both naan as directed. Either way works great.

» Fontina is a cheese that is perfect for melting. Of course, you could substitute Gruyère or provolone for a similar flavor and yes, if you must, mozzarella would work, too.

» A food processor makes quick work of shredding cheese. For the best results, be sure the cheese is well chilled. If you wish to shred mozzarella, place the piece of mozzarella in the freezer for about 15 minutes to be sure it is well chilled before shredding.

ROASTED ASPARAGUS SALAD

Roasting asparagus is simple and brings out the flavor of the vegetable. It also maintains the delicious crisp-tender texture. Arrange the roasted asparagus on fresh salad greens and you capture a delightful contrast in flavors and textures.

4 OUNCES FRESH ASPARAGUS

3 TABLESPOONS OLIVE OIL

KOSHER SALT AND FRESHLY
    GROUND BLACK PEPPER

2 TABLESPOONS FRESH LEMON
    JUICE

1 TEASPOON HONEY

1 TEASPOON DIJON MUSTARD

1½ CUPS TORN FRESH SPRING OR
    MIXED GREENS

½ CUP TORN FRESH ARUGULA
    LEAVES

¼ CUP THINLY SLICED RED BELL
    PEPPER STRIPS

2 TABLESPOONS SHREDDED
    PARMESAN CHEESE

SERVES 2

Preheat the oven to 450°F.

Snap off the woody ends of the asparagus, and if desired, remove the scales. Place the asparagus in a gallon-size zip-top bag. Drizzle with 1 tablespoon of the olive oil. Seal the bag and massage gently to distribute the oil. Place the asparagus in a single layer on a rimmed baking sheet. Season with salt and black pepper. Roast, uncovered, for 5 to 7 minutes, or until the asparagus is tender. Set aside to cool slightly.

Whisk together the remaining 2 tablespoons olive oil, the lemon juice, honey, and Dijon mustard in a small bowl. Season with salt and black pepper.

Combine the spring greens, arugula, and red pepper in a salad bowl. Drizzle with about half of the dressing mixture and toss to coat evenly. Arrange the greens on two salad plates. Top with the roasted asparagus. Drizzle with the remaining dressing mixture. Top with the Parmesan.

TIPS:

» This salad can be doubled or tripled if you are serving guests.

» Add 1 minced clove garlic to the dressing if you enjoy the flavor of garlic.

» Asparagus ranges in size and thickness so 1 pound of asparagus can have just 12 spears, or it could have 20, 30, or more spears. For this salad, 10 to 12 very thin spears is ideal—they'll roast quickly and are attractive on the bed of greens.

» If arugula is not available or if you prefer not to use it, simply eliminate it and use 2 cups spring or mixed greens.

CARAMELIZED ONION & BACON DIP

Crisp bacon, onions, and cheese always make a winning combination! This dip makes just enough so you two can settle in and watch the big game or graze during a movie, but is easily doubled so you can invite friends to join you.

1 TABLESPOON UNSALTED BUTTER

½ LARGE SWEET YELLOW ONION, CHOPPED

1 TEASPOON WHITE WINE VINEGAR

¼ TEASPOON HOT SAUCE

⅛ TEASPOON GARLIC POWDER

KOSHER SALT AND FRESHLY GROUND BLACK PEPPER

3 SLICES BACON, COOKED UNTIL CRISP THEN CRUMBLED

1 CUP SHREDDED COLBY JACK CHEESE

⅓ CUP MAYONNAISE

TOASTED BAGUETTE SLICES, CRACKERS, OR CRISP VEGETABLES, FOR SERVING

MAKES 1 CUP

Preheat the oven to 375°F. Spray a 2-cup ovenproof ramekin or individual casserole dish with nonstick spray.

Melt the butter in a 10-inch skillet over medium heat. Add the onion and cook, stirring frequently, until very tender and golden brown, about 15 minutes. Stir in the vinegar, hot sauce, garlic powder, and salt and pepper to taste. Cook, stirring continuously, for about 30 seconds, or just until the vinegar is blended in.

Stir in the bacon, cheese, and mayonnaise. Spoon into the prepared dish and bake, uncovered, for 10 to 15 minutes, or until hot and bubbling.

Serve with toasted baguette slices or other favorite dippers.

TIPS:

» Double the recipe to feed a larger crowd.

» Would you like to trim the fat? Yes, you can substitute crisp turkey bacon and reduced-fat mayonnaise. You can use reduced-fat cheddar or Colby Jack cheese, but you might want to experiment with the brand as some melt more easily and smoothly than other brands.

CHIPOTLE BEEF SLIDERS

Spicy and sweet are a match made in heaven. Let's see, does that describe your relationship, these sliders, or both?

1 POUND LEAN GROUND BEEF

1 TABLESPOON MINCED CHIPOTLE
   PEPPER IN ADOBO SAUCE

1 TABLESPOON BARBECUE SAUCE

1 CLOVE GARLIC, MINCED

KOSHER SALT AND FRESHLY
   GROUND BLACK PEPPER

6 SLIDER BUNS, TOASTED

3 TABLESPOONS SALSA

2 SLICES BACON, COOKED UNTIL
   CRISP, CUT INTO THIRDS

1 RIPE AVOCADO, PITTED, PEELED,
   AND THINLY SLICED

SERVES 6

Stir together the ground beef, chipotle pepper, barbecue sauce, garlic, and salt and pepper to taste in a bowl. Do not overwork the beef. Shape the mixture into 6 small patties.

Preheat a grill to medium-high or allow the coals to burn down to white ash.

Cook the patties for about 5 minutes per side, or until browned and a meat thermometer inserted into the center registers 160°F. Transfer the patties to a plate and cover with aluminum foil. Let rest for 5 minutes.

Serve each patty on a slider bun. Top each with about ½ tablespoon salsa, one third of a slice of cooked bacon, and 2 slices of avocado.

TIPS:

» Alternatively, cook the beef patties in a grill pan or multi grill.

» Substitute guacamole for the sliced avocado.

» See the chipotle pepper tip in the Pulled Pork Carnitas recipe on page 22.

STEAK BITES *with* SRIRACHA BUTTER

While Steak Bites with Sriracha Butter is a great addition to any party menu, we also enjoy this as an entrée with bistro-style fried potatoes and a crisp green salad.

1 BEEF FLANK STEAK, ABOUT
  ½ POUND

MARINADE:

½ CUP BEER

2 CLOVES GARLIC, MINCED

1 TABLESPOON SRIRACHA

1 TABLESPOON PACKED BROWN
  SUGAR

½ TEASPOON GROUND CUMIN

½ TEASPOON KOSHER SALT

¼ TEASPOON COARSELY GROUND
  BLACK PEPPER

SRIRACHA BUTTER:

4 TABLESPOONS (½ STICK)
  UNSALTED BUTTER, SOFTENED

1½ TEASPOONS SRIRACHA

1 CLOVE GARLIC, MINCED

SERVES 6 AS AN APPETIZER OR 2 AS AN ENTRÉE

Place the flank steak in a zip-top bag.

MAKE THE MARINADE: Whisk together all the marinade ingredients in a small bowl. Pour the marinade mixture over the steak in the bag, seal the bag, and refrigerate for several hours or overnight.

MAKE THE SRIRACHA BUTTER: Mash together all the ingredients for the Sriracha butter with a fork in a small bowl.

Preheat a grill to medium-high or allow the coals to burn down to white ash.

Drain and discard the marinade. Grill the steak, uncovered, over direct heat, for 6 minutes. Turn the meat and grill on the second side for 5 to 7 minutes, or until a meat thermometer inserted into the center registers 145°F for medium-rare or 160°F for medium. Remove the steak from the grill, cover with aluminum foil, and let rest for 5 to 10 minutes.

Spread the steak with a thin layer of the Sriracha butter. Slice the steak very thinly against the grain. Serve the steak fanned out on a serving platter or roll up each slice and secure with a toothpick. Serve with the remaining Sriracha butter.

TIPS:

» Substitute any hot sauce for Sriracha.

» This butter adds flavor to many grilled meats including rib eye, sirloin, and chicken breasts.

» Alternatively, cook the beef in a grill pan or multi grill.

MEATBALL TAPAS

Meatball Tapas make great appetizers but we enjoy them for dinner, too. Have plenty of crusty bread on hand to mop up the sauce.

1 POUND GROUND CHUCK

1 POUND GROUND PORK

2 CLOVES GARLIC, MINCED

2 TEASPOONS GROUND CUMIN

1½ TEASPOONS HOT SMOKED
    PAPRIKA

¼ TEASPOON CAYENNE PEPPER

¼ CUP PLAIN DRY BREAD CRUMBS

1 LARGE EGG, LIGHTLY BEATEN

3 TABLESPOONS CHOPPED FRESH
    PARSLEY

KOSHER SALT AND FRESHLY
    GROUND BLACK PEPPER

3 TO 4 TABLESPOONS OLIVE OIL

1 SMALL YELLOW ONION,
    CHOPPED

1 (28-OUNCE) CAN CRUSHED
    TOMATOES

CHOPPED FRESH PARSLEY, FOR
    SERVING

CRUSTY BREAD OR, RUSTIC
    COUNTRY BREAD (OPTIONAL),
    FOR SERVING

SERVES 6 TO 8 AS TAPAS OR 4 AS AN ENTRÉE

Preheat the oven to 350°F.

Combine the ground chuck, pork, garlic, cumin, 1 teaspoon of the smoked paprika, the cayenne, bread crumbs, egg, and parsley in a bowl. Season with salt and black pepper and mix with your hands to combine; do not overmix. Form the mixture into about 25 meatballs, 1½ inches in diameter.

Heat 2 tablespoons of the oil in a 12-inch ovenproof skillet over medium-high heat. Add the meatballs to the pan, leaving space between meatballs. (Work in batches if necessary to avoid overcrowding.) Brown the meatballs on all sides.

Remove the meatballs from the skillet; add additional oil to the skillet if needed. Add the onion and cook, stirring frequently, until the onion is tender. Add the tomatoes and the remaining ½ teaspoon smoked paprika. Return the meatballs to the skillet and gently spoon the sauce over them. Transfer to the oven and bake, uncovered, for 20 to 25 minutes, or until the sauce is hot and bubbly and the meatballs register 160° F in the center.

Remove the skillet from the oven and transfer the meatballs and sauce to a serving bowl. Garnish with chopped parsley and serve with crusty bread, if desired.

TIPS:

» There are lots of varieties of paprika available today and some taste quite different from the typical commercial paprika your mom or grandma bought years ago. Paprika is actually ground sweet red peppers and the flavor can range from quite mild and sweet to hot and spicy. Paprika was a very popular spice in Hungary, so today many people think of it as Hungarian. The pods for Hungarian paprika are sun-dried but the flavor of typical Hungarian paprika can range from sweet to hot. Spanish paprika (sometimes called pimentón) can also range in flavor from mild to hot or *picante*, but it is wood-smoked and has become quite popular today for its smoky flavor.

» These meatballs are great to freeze—just thaw, heat, and serve on a busy evening. Spoon the prepared meatballs with some of the sauce into a freezer container. Cover, label, and freeze. When ready to serve, allow the meat to thaw in the refrigerator overnight or place in the refrigerator before you leave for work that day, then when ready to serve, heat in the microwave until steaming hot.

» To make the meatballs in a slow cooker, mix and brown the meatballs as directed. Spray a 4-quart slow cooker with nonstick spray. Place the browned meatballs in the slow cooker. Cook the onion in the skillet as directed. Spoon the onions, tomatoes, and remaining paprika over the meatballs. Cover and cook on low for 3 to 4 hours or on high for 1½ to 2 hours. Serve the meatballs from the slow cooker. (Set to "Warm" for serving if your slow cooker has a warm setting.)

A BLAST
FROM
THE PAST

BISTRO MEAT LOAF

When life is busy and stressful, make Bistro Meat Loaf and plan a quiet evening at home. In fact, when the days are especially crazy, Kathy and her husband, David, turn to this recipe and enjoy the comforting flavor. Accompany the meat loaf with Creamy Garlic Mashed Potatoes (page 120), light the candles, and enjoy a soothing dinner at home with your honey.

MEAT LOAF:

1 TABLESPOON UNSALTED BUTTER

⅓ CUP FINELY CHOPPED ONION

2 TABLESPOONS MILK

1 LARGE EGG

1¼ CUPS FRESH BREAD CRUMBS

1 POUND LEAN GROUND BEEF

1 TEASPOON WORCESTERSHIRE SAUCE

1 TEASPOON DIJON MUSTARD

½ TEASPOON SEASONED SALT

¼ TEASPOON FRESHLY GROUND BLACK PEPPER

TOPPING:

¼ CUP KETCHUP

2 TABLESPOONS PACKED BROWN SUGAR

½ TEASPOON DIJON MUSTARD

⅛ TEASPOON HOT SAUCE

SERVES 4

MAKE THE MEAT LOAF: Preheat the oven to 375°F. Line an 11 x 7-inch pan with aluminum foil. Spray the foil with nonstick spray.

Melt the butter in a 6-inch skillet over medium-high heat. Add the onion and cook, stirring frequently, for 3 minutes. Remove from the heat and set aside.

Whisk together the milk and egg in a large bowl. Stir in the bread crumbs and cooked onion. Add the ground beef, Worcestershire sauce, Dijon mustard, salt, and pepper. Blend until evenly mixed but do not overmix, or the meatloaf will be tough.

Divide the meat mixture in half. Shape each half into a rounded oval and place in the prepared pan. Bake, uncovered, for 25 minutes.

MEANWHILE, MAKE THE TOPPING: Stir together the ketchup, brown sugar, Dijon mustard, and hot sauce in a small bowl.

Spoon the topping evenly over the loaves. Return the loaves to the oven and continue baking, uncovered, for 20 minutes more, or until a meat thermometer inserted into the center registers 160°F. Cover loosely with aluminum foil and let rest for 5 minutes before serving.

TIPS:

» A food processor is a great way to quickly make fresh bread crumbs. Generally, 2 slices of firm-textured white bread will make the 1¼ cups bread crumbs needed for this recipe.

» If desired, do not sauté the onion. Omit the butter, chop the onion very finely, and stir it into the ground beef. Proceed as directed.

» Serve one of the small meat loaves one night. Cool, wrap, label, and freeze the second. Place the frozen meat loaf in the refrigerator the night before you plan to serve it, and when dinnertime comes, microwave it until hot. Dinner is ready!

» Make mini meat loaves in a muffin pan to trim the baking time. Mix the meat mixture as directed. Spray 8 wells of a standard muffin pan with nonstick spray. Spoon the meat mixture into the wells and press lightly to shape. Fill the remaining empty wells about half full of water. Bake, uncovered, in a preheated 350°F oven for 20 minutes. Spoon the sauce on top of each and bake for 3 to 5 minutes more, or until a meat thermometer inserted into the center registers 160°F.

» How about a meat loaf sandwich? Slice the meat loaf into 1-inch-thick slices. If slicing a hot meat loaf, let it rest for 10 to 15 minutes before slicing so it slices more easily. If chilled, slice the meat loaf, then place the slices on a microwave-safe plate. Microwave on high for 45 to 60 seconds or until hot. Stack the hot meatloaf on toasted bread and add, as desired, sliced pickles, ketchup, sliced cheddar, and/or crisp, cooked bacon. Top with a second slice of toasted bread and enjoy.

OLD-FASHIONED
BEEF ROAST *with* GRAVY

This is comfort food at its best. We believe that a chuck roast has the most flavor and will cook to perfection after pan searing. It is great baked slow in the oven or it is perfect for your slow cooker. It is a natural to pair with the Creamy Garlic Mashed Potatoes on page 120.

1 BONELESS CHUCK ROAST,
   2½ TO 3 POUNDS
½ CUP ALL-PURPOSE FLOUR
KOSHER SALT
¼ TEASPOON COARSELY GROUND
   BLACK PEPPER
2 TABLESPOONS VEGETABLE OR
   OLIVE OIL
1 MEDIUM ONION, CUT INTO
   EIGHTHS
1 TEASPOON DRY MINCED GARLIC
1 (28-OUNCE) CARTON UNSALTED
   BEEF STOCK
5 MEDIUM CARROTS, HALVED
4 TABLESPOONS (½ STICK)
   UNSALTED BUTTER
FRESHLY GROUND BLACK PEPPER

SERVES 6

Preheat the oven to 325°F.

Pat the chuck roast with paper towels to remove any excess moisture or liquid.

In a shallow bowl or a gallon size zip-top bag, combine ¼ cup of the flour, ½ teaspoon salt, and the coarsely ground pepper. Place the roast in the bowl and coat with the flour mixture on all sides.

Heat the oil in a Dutch oven or deep 12-inch ovenproof skillet with a lid over medium-high heat. Add the roast and brown in the hot oil until crisp on all sides.

Remove the pan from the heat. Nestle the onion wedges around the roast. Sprinkle the garlic over the roast. Pour the beef stock over the roast. Place the carrots around the sides of the roast and submerge in the liquid. Cover and bake for 2½ to 3 hours, or until the roast is tender.

Transfer the roast to a serving platter and cover loosely with aluminum foil. Use a slotted spoon to transfer the carrots and onion to a serving bowl. Cover the vegetables loosely with foil. If the cooking liquid has a lot of debris, strain it through a fine sieve into a bowl and return the liquid to the Dutch oven, discarding any solids in the sieve.

Place the butter in a 2-cup microwave-safe glass bowl. Microwave on high for 30 seconds or until the butter is melted. Stir in the remaining ¼ cup flour, blending until smooth.

Place the Dutch oven over medium-high heat. Whisk the butter-flour mixture into the liquid in the pan. Cook, stirring continuously, until thick and smooth. Add salt and pepper to taste.

Serve the roast and vegetables with the gravy.

TIPS:

» If you prefer a crisper carrot using the oven method, add the carrots after 1 to 1½ hours of baking.

» Leftovers? No problem. Cut the meat into bite-size pieces and add the vegetables and gravy. Refrigerate or freeze. Heat and serve over hot cooked egg noodles as beef roast ragù.

» If you don't prefer a thick, rich gravy omit the gravy preparation and serve with au jus drippings.

» To make the roast in a slow cooker, spray a 4-quart slow cooker with nonstick spray. Follow the directions above, except brown the roast in a skillet and transfer to the slow cooker, omitting the beef stock and adding 1 (14.5-ounce) can reduced-sodium beef broth. Cover and cook on low for 7 to 9 hours. Remove the roast and vegetables as directed. Prepare the gravy as directed but leave the drippings in the slow cooker: Stir in the butter-flour mixture and turn the slow cooker to high for 30 minutes, stirring every 10 minutes, until the gravy is smooth and thick.

BEEF STROGANOFF STIR-FRY

This blast from the past equates to fast flavor that will comfort your souls on a chilly night. Serve with a glass of wine and a crisp green salad.

1 TABLESPOON CANOLA OR
   VEGETABLE OIL

¾ POUND TOP ROUND OR SIRLOIN
   STEAK, THINLY SLICED AGAINST
   THE GRAIN

KOSHER SALT AND FRESHLY
   GROUND BLACK PEPPER

2 TABLESPOONS UNSALTED
   BUTTER

4 OUNCES BUTTON OR WILD
   MUSHROOMS, SLICED

½ MEDIUM YELLOW ONION,
   THINLY SLICED

1 CLOVE GARLIC, MINCED

1 TABLESPOON ALL-PURPOSE
   FLOUR

1 CUP REDUCED-SODIUM BEEF
   BROTH

1 CUP SOUR CREAM

2 CUPS HOT COOKED WIDE EGG
   NOODLES, FOR SERVING

MINCED FRESH PARSLEY
   (OPTIONAL), FOR SERVING

SERVES 2

Heat the oil in a 12-inch skillet over medium-high heat. Season the sliced beef with salt and pepper. Cook the beef in the hot oil for 1 to 2 minutes on each side, or until brown. Remove from the skillet and set aside.

Reduce the heat to medium and add the butter to the skillet. Add the mushrooms and cook, stirring frequently, until the mushrooms have released their liquid, about 5 minutes. Add the onion and garlic and continue to cook, stirring frequently, for 3 to 4 minutes more.

Sprinkle the mushroom mixture with the flour and cook, stirring, for 15 seconds. Stir in the broth and bring to a simmer, scraping the bottom of the skillet to remove any browned bits. Whisk in the sour cream until the sauce is smooth. Add the beef along with any accumulated juices. Cook until the sauce comes to a simmer. Taste and adjust the salt and pepper, if necessary.

Serve over hot cooked noodles and sprinkle with parsley, if desired.

TIPS:

» Freezing meat until it is icy cold makes it easier to slice very thinly. Put the meat in the freezer for about 30 minutes, then slice. Or, if it is already frozen, place the meat in the refrigerator early in the day or before you leave for work and you will find it thawed enough to thinly slice when it's time to prepare dinner.

» Do you wonder what kind of mushrooms to use? Wild mushrooms, such as shiitake or morel mushrooms, are more flavorful and provide a deeper, earthy accent. Button mushrooms are more readily available. Use a combination of mushrooms or the variety that you prefer.

OLD-FASHIONED CHICKEN NOODLE SOUP

When cold winds are howling or you are fighting the sniffles, nothing tastes better than Old-Fashioned Chicken Noodle Soup. Snuggle together and ladle up comforting bowls of this all-time favorite homemade soup.

1½ POUNDS CHICKEN PIECES
   (SEE TIPS, PAGE 118)

2 MEDIUM CARROTS

2 MEDIUM STALKS CELERY

1 MEDIUM ONION, HALVED

1 BAY LEAF

½ TEASPOON DRIED THYME
   LEAVES

½ TEASPOON KOSHER SALT

¼ TEASPOON FRESHLY GROUND
   BLACK PEPPER

1 (32-OUNCE) CARTON REDUCED-
   SODIUM CHICKEN BROTH

2 CUPS WIDE OR EXTRA-WIDE
   NOODLES (SEE TIPS, PAGE 118)

2 TABLESPOONS MINCED FRESH
   FLAT-LEAF PARSLEY (OPTIONAL)

SERVES 6

Place the chicken in a 6-quart Dutch oven. Cut one carrot and one stalk of celery into 1½-inch pieces and add them to the chicken. Cut half of the onion into quarters and add it to the chicken. Add the bay leaf, thyme, salt, pepper, broth, and 1 cup water.

Bring to a simmer over medium-high heat. Reduce the heat to maintain a simmer, cover, and cook for 45 to 60 minutes.

Pour the soup through a fine-mesh strainer into a deep bowl. Allow the strained broth to stand for 5 to 10 minutes so the fat rises to the top; skim the fat and discard. Pour the broth back into the pan. Discard the cooked vegetables and bay leaf. When the chicken is cool enough to handle, cut the meat from the bone, discard the bones and skin, and chop the meat into bite-size pieces.

Bring a large pot of salted water to a boil for the noodles.

Stir the chopped chicken into the soup. Chop the remaining carrot, celery, and onion. Add the chopped vegetables to the soup. Heat the soup over medium-high heat until simmering. Reduce the heat to maintain a simmer, cover, and cook for 15 minutes, or until the vegetables are tender.

Cook the noodles in the boiling water according to the package directions. Drain.

Taste the soup and add additional salt and pepper, if desired. Stir in the cooked noodles. Stir in the parsley, if desired. Ladle into bowls.

(continued)

TIPS:

» The ideal chicken pieces for soup are some bone-in pieces, for depth and flavor, and some meaty pieces, so you can have chunks of meat. For this soup, you might begin with a combination of about ¾ pound bone-in chicken breasts or thighs (about 1 breast or 2 thighs) and ¾ pound boneless skinless chicken breasts. Of course, if you want to trim fat and calories, use only boneless skinless chicken breasts.

» What kind of noodles do you prefer? There is no wrong answer here. Some may enjoy thinner noodles, and others may choose "wide" or "extra-wide." What kind of noodles remind you most of Mom or Grandma?

» Why cook the noodles in a separate pot? This keeps the starch out of the soup so the soup tastes wonderful. It also happens to be a convenient way to keep leftover soup from becoming too thick and the noodles too mushy. If you do not anticipate serving all of the soup at once, divide the soup before adding the noodles, reserving half of the soup for another day. Stir freshly cooked noodles into the hot cooked soup and enjoy. Cover and refrigerate the reserved soup. When ready to serve the reserved soup, heat the soup and, separately, cook noodles for it. Add the cooked noodles to the hot soup and it will taste fresh and wonderful. Yes, if you prefer and if you are serving all of the soup at once, you can cook the noodles in the boiling soup during the last 10 minutes.

» This soup freezes well—especially if you freeze it without noodles. Spoon the soup into a freezer container, cover, label, and freeze. When ready to serve, allow it to thaw in the refrigerator overnight, then spoon the thawed soup into a 4-quart saucepan. Heat the soup until it boils, add freshly cooked noodles and 1 table-spoon minced parsley, and serve. It will taste fresh and the noodles will be perfect.

» To make the soup in a slow cooker, spray a 4-quart slow cooker with nonstick spray. Make the stock as directed, placing the chicken, chunks of vegetables, bay leaf, thyme, salt and pepper, and 1 carton of chicken broth in the slow cooker. Omit the water. Cover and cook on low for 6 to 8 hours. Strain the broth and return to the slow cooker as directed. Stir in the chopped vegetables and chopped chicken. Cover and cook on low for 3 to 5 hours or on high for 1 hour, or until vegetables are tender. Cook the noodles and stir them into the soup as directed.

CREAMY GARLIC MASHED POTATOES

This recipe is a showstopping staple that is guaranteed to round out many a menu. Search no more—these are the perfect mashed potatoes. This is the recipe you will be turning to when you celebrate your twenty-fifth wedding anniversary . . . guaranteed!

2½ POUNDS YUKON GOLD
    POTATOES, PEELED AND CUT
    INTO 1-INCH CUBES
4 CLOVES GARLIC
¼ CUP HALF-AND-HALF
1 TEASPOON KOSHER SALT
DASH OF FRESHLY GROUND
    WHITE PEPPER
¼ CUP SOUR CREAM

SERVES 6

Place the potatoes and garlic in a 4-quart saucepan and add water to cover. Bring to a boil , uncovered, over medium-high heat. Reduce the heat to maintain a gentle boil and cook for 15 to 20 minutes, or until very tender. Drain well.

Mash the potatoes. Pour the half-and-half into a small microwave-safe glass cup. Microwave on high for 30 seconds. Add the hot half-and-half to the potatoes in small amounts and beat until fluffy.

Add the remaining ingredients and mash until light and fluffy.

TIPS:

» Tools to use to mash potatoes: A potato ricer is a great tool to use to ensure fluffy, evenly mashed potatoes. To use it, put some of the cooked potatoes into the reservoir of the ricer and hold it over a bowl. Push the handle down so the potatoes are extruded through the holes. You may have to work in batches, but it is quick and easy to use. A classic alternative is a potato masher, a handheld tool with a flat surface for mashing. This works fine, but takes a little patience and effort. Electric mixers make quick work of mashing the potatoes, especially if you want light, fluffy, whipped potatoes. A food processor is not recommended as the potatoes will become pasty.

» White or black pepper? You can use either, depending on what you have available. White pepper is often suggested when making light colored foods, such as mashed potatoes, so the finished dish is more attractive. If you do not have white pepper, substitute black pepper for flavor.

» Are you not in the mood for garlic flavor? Just omit it!

» The key to great mashed potatoes is full-flavor, full-fat products. That said, you could substitute milk for the half-and-half and light or nonfat sour cream for the regular sour cream.

ULTIMATE MAC & CHEESE

Nothing tastes more comforting after a rough day than macaroni and cheese. Surprise your sweetie with this comforting dish after a busy day and enjoy a quiet evening together.

3 TABLESPOONS UNSALTED
  BUTTER, PLUS MORE FOR THE
  BAKING DISH

4 OUNCES ELBOW MACARONI

3 TABLESPOONS PANKO BREAD
  CRUMBS

3 TABLESPOONS SHREDDED
  PARMESAN CHEESE

¼ TEASPOON GARLIC SALT

2 TABLESPOONS ALL-PURPOSE
  FLOUR

1¼ CUPS MILK

½ TEASPOON DIJON MUSTARD

¼ TEASPOON KOSHER SALT

¼ TEASPOON FRESHLY GROUND
  WHITE PEPPER

1 CUP SHREDDED SHARP CHEDDAR
  CHEESE

½ CUP SHREDDED SWISS CHEESE

SERVES 4

Preheat the oven to 375°F. Butter a 1-quart casserole dish. Bring a large pot of salted water to a boil.

Cook the macaroni in boiling water according to the package directions until just tender. (Do not overcook.) Drain and set aside.

Place 1 tablespoon of the butter in a small microwave-safe glass bowl. Microwave on high for 20 to 30 seconds, or until the butter is melted. Stir in the bread crumbs, Parmesan, and garlic salt. Set aside.

Melt the remaining 2 tablespoons butter in a 3-quart saucepan over medium-high heat. Stir in the flour, blending to make a smooth paste and cook, stirring continuously, for 1 minute. Pour in about one third of the milk and cook, stirring continuously, until the mixture is smooth. Gradually stir in the remaining milk. Cook, stirring continuously, until the mixture begins to bubble and thicken. Reduce the heat to low. Stir in the Dijon mustard, kosher salt, and pepper. Stir in the cheddar and Swiss cheeses and cook, stirring continuously, until the cheeses have melted.

Remove from the heat and stir in the cooked, drained macaroni. Pour the mixture into the prepared dish. Sprinkle the reserved panko-Parmesan mixture over the top.

Bake, uncovered, for 20 minutes, or until golden.

TIPS:

» Double the recipe so you can feed your friends or take the dish to a potluck party. Use a 2-quart casserole dish or an 11 x 7-inch baking dish.

» Add 2 slices cooked and crumbled bacon when you add the macaroni to the cheese sauce. Bake as directed.

» White or black pepper? You can use either, depending on what you have available. White pepper is often suggested when making light colored foods, such as the white sauce for macaroni and cheese, so the finished dish is more attractive. If you do not have white pepper, substitute black pepper for flavor.

» Panko are dry, crisp, light bread crumbs—and are distinctive because they are coarser then typical dry bread crumbs. Once popular in Japanese cooking, they are now mainstream and common in many cooking styles. Look for canisters of panko bread crumbs on the grocery shelves by typical dry bread crumbs or in the Asian foods section.

DESSERTS &
INDULGENCES

CHOCOLATE PEANUT BUTTER PIE
with CHOCOLATE PRETZEL CRUST

This pie is such a treat, and the sweet, salty flavor combined with chocolate and peanut butter will remind you of candy. Surprise the love of your life and make this fantastic dessert tonight!

CRUST:

1½ CUPS BROKEN SMALL
    PRETZEL STICKS

2 TABLESPOONS PACKED BROWN
    SUGAR

½ CUP SEMISWEET CHOCOLATE
    CHIPS

2 TABLESPOONS UNSALTED
    BUTTER, MELTED

CHOCOLATE FILLING:

1½ CUPS SEMISWEET CHOCOLATE
    CHIPS

6 TABLESPOONS HEAVY CREAM

½ TEASPOON PURE VANILLA
    EXTRACT

MAKES 1 (9-INCH) PIE

MAKE THE CRUST: Preheat the oven to 375°F.

Place the pretzels in a zip-top bag. Crush the pretzel sticks to form even, coarse crumbs. Pour the pretzel crumbs into a small bowl. Stir in the brown sugar, chocolate chips, and butter. Spoon the pretzel mixture into a 9-inch pie pan. Use the back of the spoon to pack lightly. Bake for 10 minutes. Set aside and allow to cool completely.

MAKE THE CHOCOLATE FILLING: Combine the chocolate chips and cream in a small microwave-safe glass bowl. Microwave on high for 60 to 90 seconds, or until the cream comes to a boil, stirring midway through. Stir until the chocolate chips are melted and the mixture is smooth. Stir in the vanilla. Set aside.

MAKE THE PEANUT BUTTER FILLING: Whisk together the granulated sugar and cornstarch in a 2-quart saucepan. (Whisking until the two are blended together helps avoid lumps.) Whisk together the milk and egg yolks in a small bowl. Pour the milk–egg yolk mixture into the sugar mixture in the saucepan and whisk until combined. Cook over medium heat, whisking continuously, until the mixture begins to thicken and comes to a boil. Continue to cook, whisking continuously, for 1 minute. Remove from the heat and stir in the peanut butter and vanilla.

PEANUT BUTTER FILLING:

⅔ CUP GRANULATED SUGAR

2 TABLESPOONS CORNSTARCH

1⅓ CUPS MILK

2 LARGE EGG YOLKS

½ CUP CREAMY PEANUT BUTTER

1 TEASPOON PURE VANILLA
 EXTRACT

TO ASSEMBLE:

1 CUP HEAVY CREAM

2 TABLESPOONS CONFECTIONERS'
 SUGAR

ASSEMBLE THE PIE: Spoon about ⅓ cup of the chocolate filling into a small microwave-safe glass bowl, cover, and set aside. Spoon the remaining chocolate filling into the crust, using the back of a spoon to smooth it gently to cover the crust. Spoon the peanut butter filling evenly over the chocolate filling, using the back of a spoon to smooth it gently. Cover the pie lightly with plastic wrap, pressing very gently so the plastic touches the peanut butter filling. Refrigerate for at least 1 hour, or until the filling is chilled and set, or overnight. (If chilling overnight, cover and refrigerate the reserved chocolate filling as well.)

Gently lift the plastic off the pie. Beat the cream in a small, deep bowl, using a handheld electric mixer at medium speed, until the cream is frothy. Gradually beat in the confectioners' sugar and continue beating until stiff peaks form. Pipe or dollop the whipped cream over the pie in a decorative fashion.

Microwave the reserved chocolate filling on high for 30 seconds, or until warm and the chocolate flows easily from the tip of a spoon, stirring midway through. Spoon the warm chocolate into a zip-top bag and seal. Snip one corner off the bag and drizzle the melted chocolate decoratively over the pie.

(continued)

TIPS:

» Store leftover pie in the refrigerator for up to 3 days.

» A rolling pin or the flat edge of a meat tenderizer are both convenient tools to use to crush the pretzels into crumbs.

» One 12-ounce package of semisweet chocolate chips will give the amount of chips needed for this pie.

» To make two (4¼-inch) individual pies, cut all the ingredient quantities in half and use a 6-ounce package of chocolate chips. Prepare as directed, spreading the crust evenly over the bottom of two individual (4¼ x 1½-inch) pie pans. Bake for 10 minutes. Assemble the pies as directed, dividing the fillings and toppings evenly between the two crusts.

» If desired, omit the whipped cream and substitute frozen whipped topping, thawed.

» If desired, add chopped chocolate peanut butter cup candies as a garnish on top of the pie.

» To prepare the crust in a food processor, place the pretzels in the work bowl of a food processor and pulse until coarsely chopped, then add the brown sugar, chocolate chips, and melted butter and pulse quickly to combine. (Yes, the chocolate chips are chopped when preparing the crust in a food processor, but are not chopped when stirred together. It is not a problem, for the chips melt when the crust is baked.)

SUMMER FRUIT GALETTE

Nothing says summer like fresh peaches and blueberries. Your friends will think you are a trained pastry chef, and you won't be stressed preparing this simple yet elegant fruit galette, a type of freeform tart.

1¼ CUPS ALL-PURPOSE FLOUR

¼ CUP GRANULATED SUGAR

¼ TEASPOON TABLE SALT

8 TABLESPOONS (1 STICK) COLD
   UNSALTED BUTTER, CUT INTO
   SMALL CUBES

¼ CUP ICE WATER

3 LARGE FRESH PEACHES, PEELED,
   PITTED, AND THINLY SLICED

1 CUP FRESH BLUEBERRIES

¼ CUP PACKED BROWN SUGAR

½ TEASPOON GROUND
   CINNAMON

SERVES 6

Place the flour, granulated sugar, and salt in the work bowl of a food processor and pulse to combine. Add the butter and pulse until the butter is evenly cut into the mixture and it resembles coarse crumbs. Sprinkle with the ice water and continue to pulse just until the mixture comes together into a ball. Do not overwork. Gather the dough into a ball and flatten it into a disc. Wrap the dough in plastic wrap and refrigerate for at least 30 minutes or overnight.

Preheat the oven to 425°F. Line a rimmed baking sheet with parchment paper.

Place the prepared crust on a lightly floured work surface and roll it to form a 12-inch circle. Carefully place the dough on the prepared baking sheet.

Combine the peaches and blueberries in a medium bowl. Toss with the brown sugar and cinnamon. Mound the peach mixture in the center of the dough, leaving 2 inches around the border. Fold the edges up and overlap around the peaches.

Bake for 45 to 50 minutes, or until the crust is golden and the peaches are bubbling. Let cool for 15 to 20 minutes before serving.

TIPS:

» This can be made a few hours ahead and served at room temperature or warmed in the oven.

» Hungering for peaches in the dead of winter? Substitute 1 (16-ounce) package frozen, sliced peaches and 1 cup frozen blueberries for fresh ingredients. No need to thaw the fruit.

BERRY-ALMOND TARTS FOR TWO

These Berry-Almond Tarts for Two are a feast for your eyes and for your palate.

CRUST:

⅓ CUP ALL-PURPOSE FLOUR

2 TABLESPOONS SLICED ALMONDS, TOASTED

1 TABLESPOON GRANULATED SUGAR

DASH OF TABLE SALT

2 TABLESPOONS COLD UNSALTED BUTTER, CUT INTO SMALL PIECES

2 TO 3 TEASPOONS ICE WATER

FILLING:

3 OUNCES CREAM CHEESE, SOFTENED

2 TABLESPOONS SOUR CREAM

2 TABLESPOONS GRANULATED SUGAR

¼ TEASPOON PURE ALMOND EXTRACT

1 CUP FRESH SLICED STRAWBERRIES, RASPBERRIES, BLUEBERRIES, OR A COMBINATION

2 TABLESPOONS STRAWBERRY OR SEEDLESS RASPBERRY PRESERVES

2 TABLESPOONS SLICED ALMONDS, TOASTED

SERVES 2

MAKE THE CRUST: Place the flour, almonds, sugar, and salt in the work bowl of a food processor and process until the almonds are finely chopped. Add the butter and pulse until the butter is evenly cut into the mixture and the mixture resembles coarse crumbs. Sprinkle with 2 teaspoons of the ice water and continue to pulse just until the mixture comes together into a ball. Do not overwork. If the dough is still dry, add additional ice water ½ teaspoon at a time, until the dough holds together. Wrap the dough in plastic wrap and refrigerate for several hours or overnight.

Preheat the oven to 375°F.

Place the prepared crust on a lightly floured work surface and roll it very thin, about ⅛ inch thick. Cut two circles, each about 5½ to 6 inches in diameter. (To make a guide, invert a tart pan, about 4½ x ¾ inch, on the dough to estimate the needed size. With the tip of a sharp knife, trace about ¾ inch outside the edge of the tart pan.) Gently lift up one crust circle using a pancake turner and place it in a tart pan. Use your fingertips to flatten the crust, covering the bottom and sides of the tart pan. Repeat with the second circle. (If necessary, reroll scraps to cut the circle for the second tart pan.) Using the tines of a fork, prick the crusts evenly all over. Bake for 11 to 12 minutes, or until the crusts are set and very lightly golden in color. Place on a wire rack and allow to cool completely.

MEANWHILE, MAKE THE FILLING: Beat together the cream cheese, sour cream, sugar, and almond extract in a small bowl, using a handheld electric mixer at medium speed, until smooth. Divide the filling evenly between the crusts. Spread evenly to fill each crust.

(continued)

Top each tart with berries.

Spoon the preserves into a small microwave-safe glass bowl. Microwave on high for 30 seconds, or until the preserves are melted. Slowly spoon the preserves over the berries, covering completely. Garnish with almonds.

Serve immediately or cover and refrigerate for up to 2 days.

TIPS:

» Toast ¼ cup almonds so you can use 2 tablespoons for the crust and 2 tablespoons for the garnish. Toasting the almonds intensifies their flavor. To toast the almonds, spread the almonds in a single layer on a baking sheet. Toast in a preheated 350°F oven for 5 to 7 minutes, or until golden.

» Use your favorite berries or choose a variety of raspberries, blueberries, and blackberries. If you choose strawberries, choose small berries or halve or slice larger berries.

CHOCOLATE CHOCOLATE CHIP COOKIES

We believe that every newlywed couple needs to own a cookie jar. Vintage cookie jars bring back nostalgic memories and can be purchased at thrift stores and flea markets. Invest in a cookie jar that is sure to become a family heirloom for years to come, and then christen your new purchase with a batch of these Chocolate Chocolate Chip Cookies.

8 TABLESPOONS (1 STICK)
  UNSALTED BUTTER, SOFTENED
½ CUP GRANULATED SUGAR
½ CUP PACKED BROWN SUGAR
1 LARGE EGG
1 TEASPOON PURE VANILLA
  EXTRACT
1 CUP ALL-PURPOSE FLOUR
⅓ CUP UNSWEETENED COCOA
  POWDER
1 TEASPOON BAKING SODA
¼ TEASPOON TABLE SALT
1 CUP SEMISWEET CHOCOLATE
  CHIPS

MAKES 24 COOKIES

Preheat the oven to 375°F. Line two baking sheets with parchment paper.

Beat together the butter, granulated sugar, and brown sugar in a large bowl, using a handheld electric mixer at medium-high speed, until the mixture is light and fluffy. Beat in the egg and vanilla.

Whisk together the flour, cocoa, baking soda, and salt in a small bowl. Add to the butter mixture and mix until just combined. (Do not overmix.) Stir in the chocolate chips.

Use a cookie scoop to drop heaping tablespoons of the cookie dough about 2 inches apart onto the prepared baking sheets. Bake for 9 to 11 minutes or until set. (Do not overbake.) Let cool for 1 minute, then transfer to a wire rack to cool completely.

TIPS:

» Replace the semisweet chocolate chips with white chocolate chips, peanut butter chips, or mint-flavored chips.

» Add ½ cup toasted chopped pecans to the cookies, stirring in the nuts when you add the chocolate chips. Toasting the pecans intensifies their flavor. To toast the pecans, spread the pecans in a single layer on a baking sheet. Toast in a preheated 350°F oven for 5 to 7 minutes, or until golden.

KILLER BROWNIES

A wonderful way to "smother" your spouse with love. Brownies that are oozing with caramel will make any occasion romantic.

12 TABLESPOONS (1½ STICKS) UNSALTED BUTTER

1½ CUPS GRANULATED SUGAR

3 LARGE EGGS, BEATEN

2 TEASPOONS PURE VANILLA EXTRACT

½ TEASPOON TABLE SALT

½ TEASPOON BAKING POWDER

1 CUP ALL-PURPOSE FLOUR

½ CUP UNSWEETENED COCOA POWDER

½ CUP PECAN PIECES, TOASTED

1 (11-OUNCE) PACKAGE CARAMEL BITS

⅓ CUP HEAVY CREAM OR HALF-AND-HALF

MAKES 16 (2-INCH) BROWNIES

Preheat the oven to 350°F. Line an 8 x 8 x 2-inch baking pan with nonstick aluminum foil or parchment paper. Spray the bottom only with nonstick spray.

Melt the butter in a 4-quart saucepan over medium-high heat. Remove from the heat and stir in the sugar. Allow to cool slightly.

Add the eggs and vanilla and stir until blended. Stir in the salt and baking powder. Add the flour and cocoa powder and stir until the batter is smooth, but do not overstir. Stir in the pecans.

Pour half of the batter into the prepared pan. Bake for 15 minutes.

Meanwhile, combine the caramel bits and heavy cream in a 4-cup microwave-safe glass bowl. Microwave on high for 1½ to 2 minutes, stirring in 30-second intervals, until the caramel is melted.

Pour the melted caramel mixture over the baked brownie. Dollop the remaining batter evenly over the top of the caramel layer to form another brownie layer. Bake for an additional 25 to 27 minutes, or until softly set. (Do not overbake; a toothpick inserted in the center will come out moist due to the caramel sauce.)

Let cool on a wire rack for at least 4 hours. Carefully lift the brownies from the pan and peel away the foil from the sides. Cut into squares with a sharp knife.

Store in an airtight container at room temperature for up to 4 days.

(continued)

KILLER BROWNIES *(continued)*

TIPS:

» For easier cutting, heat the knife by placing it under very hot water and wiping it dry before cutting. Rinse the knife under very hot water several times in between cuts.

» Toasting the pecans intensifies their flavor. To toast the pecans, spread the pecans in a single layer on a baking sheet. Toast in a preheated 350°F oven for 5 to 7 minutes, or until golden.

» If desired, omit the pecans.

» This is one time when nonstick aluminum foil is needed. Allow the brownies to cool for at least 4 hours before cutting—this allows the caramel to firm up, which will cause it to stick to regular aluminum foil.

PEANUT BUTTER JAM JEWELS

Do you like peanut butter and jelly sandwiches? These cookies capture those all-time favorite flavors and the jewel-toned red jam in the center of the cookie shines like a beautiful gem.

1 CUP CREAMY PEANUT BUTTER

8 TABLESPOONS (1 STICK) UNSALTED BUTTER, SOFTENED

2/3 CUP PACKED BROWN SUGAR

1 LARGE EGG

1 TEASPOON PURE VANILLA EXTRACT

1 1/3 CUPS ALL-PURPOSE FLOUR

1 TEASPOON BAKING SODA

1/2 TEASPOON TABLE SALT

1/4 CUP GRANULATED SUGAR

1/3 CUP STRAWBERRY JAM (OR WHATEVER FLAVOR YOU PREFER)

MAKES ABOUT 36 COOKIES

Preheat the oven to 350°F. Line two baking sheets with parchment paper.

Beat together the peanut butter, butter, and brown sugar in a large bowl, using a handheld electric mixer at medium-high speed, until the mixture is light and fluffy. Beat in the egg and vanilla.

Whisk together the flour, baking soda, and salt in a small bowl. Add to the butter mixture and mix until just combined. (Do not overmix.) Cover and refrigerate the dough for 1 hour, or until chilled.

Pour the granulated sugar into a shallow bowl. Shape the dough into 1-inch balls using about 1 tablespoon of dough for each. Roll each ball in the granulated sugar. Place the dough balls about 2 inches apart on the prepared baking sheets. Using the end of a wooden spoon dipped in the sugar, indent the center of each ball, making a circle about 1/2 inch in diameter and 3/4 inch deep.

Bake for 10 to 12 minutes, or until just set and very lightly golden brown. Transfer to a wire rack and let cool completely.

Just before serving, spoon the jam into a small microwave-safe glass cup or bowl. Microwave on high for 20 to 30 seconds, or until melted.

Spoon about 1/2 teaspoon of the hot jam into the indentation in each cookie.

TIPS:

» To maintain the best texture, melt the jam and fill the cookies just before serving. Store unfilled cookies in an airtight container at room temperature for up to 3 days.

ENTERTAINING

BUFFALO CHICKEN RICE BAKE

This is not your mother's chicken and rice casserole—this version has definitely been kicked up a notch. It is ideal to make and share when friends gather or you want to contribute to the potluck. Not sure buffalo flavor is for you? Read the Tip below for a south-of-the-border version.

1 CUP REDUCED-SODIUM CHICKEN
   BROTH OR WATER
½ CUP UNCOOKED LONG-GRAIN
   WHITE RICE
1 TABLESPOON OLIVE OIL
1 POUND BONELESS SKINLESS
   CHICKEN BREASTS, CUT INTO
   BITE-SIZE CUBES
2 MEDIUM STALKS CELERY, THINLY
   SLICED
½ CUP CHOPPED YELLOW ONION
1 (14.5-OUNCE) CAN PETITE DICED
   TOMATOES, WITH LIQUID
½ CUP BUFFALO WING SAUCE
¼ CUP BLEU CHEESE CRUMBLES

SERVES 4

Preheat the oven to 375°F. Spray an 8-inch square baking dish with nonstick spray.

Bring the chicken broth to a boil in a 1-quart saucepan over medium-high heat. Stir in the rice and reduce the heat to maintain a simmer. Cover and simmer for 15 to 20 minutes, or until the broth is absorbed and the rice is done.

Heat the olive oil in a 12-inch nonstick skillet over medium-high heat. Add the chicken, celery, and onion. Cook for 6 to 8 minutes, stirring frequently, until the chicken is cooked through and the onion is tender. Add the tomatoes with their juices and the wing sauce to the chicken mixture; stir to combine.

Spoon the cooked rice evenly into the prepared baking dish. Spoon the chicken mixture over the rice (do not stir). Bake, uncovered, for 20 minutes. Sprinkle evenly with the bleu cheese and continue to bake for 5 to 10 minutes more, or until the center is hot and a thermometer inserted in the center registers 165°F. Serve hot.

TIPS:

» Prepare as directed, except substitute salsa for the buffalo sauce and substitute shredded cheddar cheese for the bleu cheese.

EASY-PEASY GARLIC TOAST

This is a classic, and just about any time you serve a pasta dish in the United States, the natural accompaniment is crusty garlic toast. Easy-Peasy Garlic Toast may be easy, but it is packed with flavor.

1 LOAF ITALIAN OR CIABATTA
   BREAD
6 TABLESPOONS (¾ STICK)
   UNSALTED BUTTER, SOFTENED
3 TO 4 CLOVES GARLIC, MINCED
KOSHER SALT AND FRESHLY
   GROUND BLACK PEPPER
2 TABLESPOONS MINCED FRESH
   FLAT-LEAF PARSLEY

SERVES 6

Preheat the oven to 350°F.

Split the bread loaf in half lengthwise. Place each half, cut-side up, on a baking sheet.

Stir together the butter, garlic, salt and pepper to taste, and the parsley in a small bowl. Spread the butter mixture evenly over the bread.

Bake for 12 to 15 minutes, or until hot and lightly browned.

Cut each half into thick slices. Serve warm.

TIPS:

» Try cheesy garlic bread: Stir 1 cup shredded mozzarella cheese and ¼ cup shredded Parmesan cheese into the butter. Spread on the bread and bake as directed.

» If desired, add 1 teaspoon Italian seasoning to the butter or substitute minced fresh basil for the parsley.

PENNE IN HERBED BRIE SAUCE
with MUSHROOMS & SPINACH

Invite your friends for a dinner party! Penne in Herbed Brie Sauce with Mushrooms and Spinach lets you entertain in style and not break the bank.

12 OUNCES PENNE

2 TABLESPOONS OLIVE OIL

1 MEDIUM SWEET YELLOW ONION, CHOPPED

8 OUNCES BUTTON OR WILD MUSHROOMS, SLICED

3 CLOVES GARLIC, MINCED

¾ CUP DRY WHITE WINE

1 TEASPOON DRIED BASIL LEAVES

KOSHER SALT AND FRESHLY GROUND BLACK PEPPER

2 CUPS FRESH, TRIMMED SPINACH LEAVES, COARSELY CHOPPED

1 (7-OUNCE) WEDGE BRIE, TRIMMED OF RIND AND CUT INTO ½-INCH CUBES (SEE TIPS, PAGE 144)

½ CUP HEAVY CREAM

2 TABLESPOONS MINCED FRESH BASIL, PLUS FRESH BASIL LEAVES (OPTIONAL), FOR SERVING

SERVES 6

Bring a large pot of salted water to a boil and cook the penne according to the package directions. Drain and set aside.

Heat the olive oil in a 12-inch nonstick skillet over medium-high heat. Cook the onion for 3 minutes, stirring frequently. Stir in the mushrooms and cook, stirring continuously, for 4 to 5 minutes, or until the onions and mushrooms are tender and the liquid has evaporated. Stir in the garlic and cook for 30 seconds.

Reduce the heat to low. Stir in the wine, dried basil leaves, and salt and pepper to taste. Stir in the spinach and cook for 1 minute, stirring continuously. Stir in the Brie and the cream, and stir until the Brie has melted and the sauce is smooth and begins to bubble. Stir in the cooked pasta.

Spoon into a large serving bowl and sprinkle with the minced fresh basil. Toss to combine. Garnish with fresh basil leaves, if desired.

(continued)

TIPS:

» Can you eat the rind on Brie? Sure, and many feel it is the best part. However, the texture of the rind varies—sometimes it is dry and leathery, and other times, thin and softer. To be sure the sauce is smooth and all of the cheese melts evenly, trim away the rind, especially if it is dry or leathery.

» This versatile dish is a great vegetarian main dish, or serve it as a side dish and accompany it with grilled or roasted chicken or pork. If you would like meat in this pasta dish, stir in 4 slices bacon or pancetta, cooked until crisp then crumbled, or 1 to 2 cups cooked cubed chicken or grilled shrimp just before serving.

» What is a serving of pasta? Many restaurants serve such large portions that we forget that 2 ounces of pasta is considered a standard serving. If you are preparing this recipe to serve as a main dish for six hearty eaters, you might want to double the recipe, sautéing the onions and mushrooms in a Dutch oven.

» If desired, sprinkle with shredded Parmesan cheese just before serving.

CHICKEN PAILLARDS *with* GREENS & PEPPERED PARMESAN DRESSING

There is no need to fuss or worry when your in-laws come to dinner. When they do, serve this delicious dish. They will be impressed with how good it tastes and how easily and quickly you prepared it. Since this dish features both meat and salad in one dish, just accompany with crusty bread and dinner is served.

CHICKEN PAILLARDS:

4 BONELESS SKINLESS CHICKEN
   BREAST HALVES, ABOUT
   6 OUNCES EACH

¼ CUP OLIVE OIL

¼ CUP FRESH LEMON JUICE

2 CLOVES GARLIC, MINCED

2 TABLESPOONS DIJON MUSTARD

KOSHER SALT AND FRESHLY
   GROUND BLACK PEPPER

PEPPERED PARMESAN DRESSING:

¼ CUP LIGHT MAYONNAISE

3 TABLESPOONS FRESH LEMON
   JUICE

2 CLOVES GARLIC, MINCED

½ TEASPOON COARSELY GROUND
   BLACK PEPPER

KOSHER SALT

3 TABLESPOONS OLIVE OIL

⅓ CUP SHREDDED PARMESAN
   CHEESE

TO ASSEMBLE:

1½ TO 2 CUPS TORN ARUGULA
   LEAVES OR SPRING SALAD GREENS

SHREDDED PARMESAN CHEESE

COARSELY GROUND BLACK PEPPER

SERVES 4

MAKE THE CHICKEN PAILLARDS: Pound the chicken breasts between sheets of plastic wrap until the chicken is very thin, about ¼ inch thick. Place the chicken in a zip-top bag.

Stir together the olive oil, lemon juice, garlic, Dijon mustard, and salt and pepper to taste in a small bowl. Pour the olive oil mixture over chicken. Seal the bag and massage to coat the chicken evenly. Refrigerate for 30 minutes.

Preheat a grill to medium-high or allow the coals to burn down to white ash.

Grill the chicken for 2 to 3 minutes per side, or until the meat is browned and no longer pink inside and a meat thermometer inserted into the center registers 165°F. Transfer the chicken to a platter, cover with aluminum foil, and let rest for 5 minutes.

MAKE THE PEPPERED PARMESAN DRESSING: Whisk together the mayonnaise, lemon juice, garlic, pepper, and salt to taste in a small bowl. While whisking, slowly drizzle in the olive oil and continue whisking until combined. Whisk in the shredded Parmesan.

ASSEMBLE THE DISH: Arrange the arugula on the center of each chicken breast. Drizzle with the dressing. Garnish with additional shredded Parmesan and pepper.

PORK MEDALLIONS *with* SAGE & MUSHROOM SAUCE

This dish is elegant with flavor that rivals a five-star restaurant. The sauce is divine and would be equally delicious with boneless skinless chicken breasts.

1½ POUNDS PORK TENDERLOIN, SLICED CROSSWISE 1½ INCHES THICK

2 TABLESPOONS OLIVE OIL

8 OUNCES BABY BELLA MUSHROOMS, SLICED

3 CLOVES GARLIC, MINCED

2 TABLESPOONS ALL-PURPOSE FLOUR

1¼ CUPS LOW-SODIUM CHICKEN BROTH

2 TABLESPOONS WHITE WINE VINEGAR

2 TABLESPOONS FRESH LEMON JUICE

2 TABLESPOONS MINCED FRESH SAGE

2 TABLESPOONS MINCED FRESH FLAT-LEAF PARSLEY, PLUS ADDITIONAL FRESH ITALIAN PARSLEY LEAVES FOR SERVING

KOSHER SALT AND FRESHLY GROUND BLACK PEPPER

Pound the pork between sheets of plastic wrap until about 1 inch thick.

Heat the olive oil in a 12-inch skillet over medium-high heat. Add the pork and cook until browned on both sides and almost cooked through, 5 to 7 minutes. Remove the pork from the skillet and set aside.

Add the mushrooms to the skillet and cook, stirring frequently, for 5 minutes. Add the garlic and cook, stirring continuously, for 30 seconds. Sprinkle the mushrooms with the flour and cook for 30 seconds, stirring to moisten the flour and coat the mushrooms evenly. Gradually stir in the broth. Cook, stirring continuously, until the broth boils. Reduce the heat to maintain a simmer. Continue to cook, stirring continuously, until the mixture thickens. Stir in the vinegar and lemon juice. Add the minced sage and parsley.

Return the pork to the skillet and simmer until the pork is cooked through and a meat thermometer inserted in the center registers 155°F. Season with salt and pepper. Sprinkle with parsley before serving.

TIPS:

» Substitute any variety of mushroom for the baby bella mushrooms (these are also known as cremini mushrooms). Wild mushrooms would work nicely in this recipe as they are more flavorful and provide a deeper, earthy accent. Buttons mushrooms are readily available and provide a milder flavor.

» We like the tangy flavor added to the sauce by the lemon juice. If you don't have fresh lemon juice, you could eliminate it.

» The sauce on this pork is very flavorful and we enjoy serving it accompanied by hot cooked pasta, rice, couscous, or mashed potatoes.

PHYLLO-WRAPPED BEEF TENDERLOIN

Is it time for romance? There is no finer way to celebrate your anniversary or that new job than with this recipe. Yet, there is no need to wait for an excuse to celebrate—just set aside an evening as a special date night. Best of all, you can assemble the beef wrapped in the pastry early in the day and refrigerate it. When dinnertime comes, pour the wine and pop it into the oven—it's that easy.

2 BEEF TENDERLOIN STEAKS 4 TO
   6 OUNCES EACH

MUSHROOM FILLING:

1 TABLESPOON UNSALTED BUTTER

4 OUNCES BUTTON OR WILD
   MUSHROOMS, STEMMED AND
   FINELY CHOPPED

1 SHALLOT, MINCED

1 CLOVE GARLIC, MINCED

1 TABLESPOON MINCED FRESH
   THYME LEAVES

KOSHER SALT AND FRESHLY
   GROUND BLACK PEPPER

TO ASSEMBLE:

1 TABLESPOON VEGETABLE OIL

KOSHER SALT AND COARSELY
   GROUND BLACK PEPPER

10 (14 X 9-INCH) SHEETS PHYLLO
   DOUGH, THAWED

4 TABLESPOONS (½ STICK)
   UNSALTED BUTTER, MELTED

SERVES 2

Set the beef out of the refrigerator for 10 to 15 minutes to allow it to come to room temperature. Preheat the oven to 400°F. Line a rimmed baking sheet with aluminum foil, then spray the foil with nonstick spray.

MAKE THE MUSHROOM FILLING: Melt the butter in a 10-inch skillet over medium heat. Add the mushrooms and shallot and cook, stirring frequently, for 5 to 6 minutes, or until the vegetables are very tender and all the liquid has evaporated. Add the garlic and cook, stirring frequently, for 30 seconds. Stir in the thyme and salt and pepper to taste and cook, stirring frequently, for 30 seconds. Remove from the heat and set aside to cool.

ASSEMBLE THE DISH: Heat the oil in a skillet (you can use the same skillet you used to cook the mushrooms) over medium high heat. Season the beef with salt and pepper. Place the beef in the hot skillet and cook for 1 to 2 minutes, or until well browned. Turn the meat and brown the second side. Turn and brown the outside edges of the steaks. Remove the beef from the skillet and set aside.

Remove the phyllo sheets from the package, unfold them, and place the sheets on a clean tray. Cover them with plastic wrap and then a damp towel to prevent drying. Remove one sheet and place it on the work surface. Brush it lightly with melted butter. Stack a second sheet of phyllo crosswise over the first and brush it with butter. Continue crisscrossing the sheets until 5 are stacked, brushing each with butter. Make a second stack in the same fashion with the remaining 5 phyllo sheets. Place a browned beef tenderloin steak in the center of each stack. Divide the mushroom mixture evenly between the tenderloin steaks, mounding as necessary so the mushrooms are on top of the meat. Fold one side of phyllo up over the meat and mushrooms. Fold each end up over the meat, smoothing gently as you go. Fold the remaining side up over the top, then smooth gently, taking care to encase all of the meat and mushrooms completely in the phyllo.

Place the pastry-wrapped meat on a baking sheet. Bake for 14 to 16 minutes, or until the pastry is golden brown and a meat thermometer inserted into the center of the meat registers 145°F for medium-rare. Remove the meat from the oven and let rest, uncovered, for 5 minutes. Carefully lift the steaks off the baking sheet and place on the dinner plates.

TIPS:

» Make-ahead convenience: Assemble as directed and place on an aluminum foil–covered baking sheet. Refrigerate, uncovered, for up to 8 hours. When ready to bake, let stand at room temperature for up to 30 minutes before baking. Bake in a preheated 400°F oven as directed above, increasing the baking time to 16 to 20 minutes, or until the pastry is browned and a meat thermometer registers 145°F for medium-rare. If the baking sheet will not fit in your refrigerator, place the pastry-wrapped beef on an aluminum foil–lined plate, then lift the foil off the plate and place both foil and beef on the baking sheet. (The unbaked pastry may stick to a tray or plate, so leave it on the foil and reposition the foil on the baking sheet, so the pastry does not tear.)

» Do you like peppercorn-crusted beef? Generously season the beef with freshly cracked black pepper.

» Beef tenderloin steaks are often called filet mignons or beef medallions. Read the label carefully, for some shops sell sirloin fillets, cut to resemble the medallion shape. Those cut from the sirloin are less expensive but will not be as tender and flavorful as medallions cut from the tenderloin. Sometimes, the medallions available are quite large and you can ask the butcher to cut them into the 4- to 6-ounce size.

GLAZED CRANBERRY CHOCOLATE CAKE

You may think that you need to be a pastry chef to construct this showstopper. Think again. The parts go together easily enough and you will be the star of the holiday buffet with this dessert.

1½ CUPS ALL-PURPOSE FLOUR

1½ CUPS GRANULATED SUGAR

¾ CUP UNSWEETENED COCOA
   POWDER

1½ TEASPOONS BAKING SODA

¾ TEASPOON BAKING POWDER

½ TEASPOON TABLE SALT

2 LARGE EGGS

¾ CUP BUTTERMILK

3 TABLESPOONS VEGETABLE OIL

1 TABLESPOON PURE VANILLA
   EXTRACT

¾ CUP HOT STRONG BREWED
   COFFEE

MAKES 1 (8-INCH) DOUBLE-LAYER CAKE

Preheat the oven to 350°F.

Butter or spray with nonstick spray two 8-inch round cake pans. Cut parchment rounds to fit and place them in the cake pans. Butter and spray the parchment.

Mix together the flour, sugar, cocoa powder, baking soda, baking powder, and salt in a large bowl, using a handheld electric mixer at low speed, until the mixture is combined. Beat in the eggs, buttermilk, oil, and vanilla, beating on medium speed for 30 seconds and scraping the sides of the bowl. Add the coffee and continue to beat for 1½ to 2 minutes, or until smooth. Divide the batter evenly between the prepared pans.

Bake for 28 to 32 minutes, or until a toothpick inserted in the center of the cake comes out clean.

Let cool on a wire rack for 10 minutes, then invert the cakes onto the racks and allow to cool completely.

(continued)

CHOCOLATE FROSTING:

8 TABLESPOONS (1 STICK)
   UNSALTED BUTTER, SOFTENED

⅓ CUP UNSWEETENED COCOA
   POWDER

3 CUPS CONFECTIONERS' SUGAR

1 TEASPOON PURE VANILLA
   EXTRACT

3 TABLESPOONS BREWED COFFEE,
   AT ROOM TEMPERATURE

GLAZED CRANBERRIES:

3 CUPS FRESH CRANBERRIES

½ CUP GRANULATED SUGAR

¾ CUP CHOPPED PECANS,
   TOASTED (OPTIONAL)

TO ASSEMBLE:

CHOCOLATE FROSTING AND
   GLAZED CRANBERRIES ON
   PAGE 152

MAKE THE CHOCOLATE FROSTING: Beat the butter in a large bowl, using a handheld electric mixer at medium-high speed, until the butter is fluffy. Add the remaining ingredients and beat until smooth and spreadable.

MAKE THE GLAZED CRANBERRIES: Place the cranberries on a rimmed baking sheet. Sprinkle with the sugar and stir well to distribute. Bake for 15 minutes at 350°, stirring every 5 minutes. Allow to cool completely.

ASSEMBLE THE CAKE: Frost the top of the bottom layer. Place the second cake layer on top of the frosting on the bottom layer and frost around the sides of the cake. Frost the top of the cake with a thin layer of frosting.

Top with the glazed cranberries. If desired, press pecans onto the sides of cake.

TIPS:

» If you want to make the cake extra fancy for a festive presentation, double the frosting recipe. Pipe the frosting around top edge of the cake, using a star tip on a pastry bag. Carefully fill the center with the glazed cranberries. Use a toothpick to arrange the cranberries.

» If this still seems intimidating, why not bake the cake layers a few days ahead, wrap each layer in plastic wrap, and freeze them? The cake is much easier to frost and work with when frozen, and it will thaw beautifully in a few hours.

» Omit the cranberries and turn to this recipe for a traditional chocolate cake with frosting.

» Cranberries may not be available year round at your grocery store, but they are easy to freeze. Just pick up an extra package of fresh cranberries in November or December when they are readily available and place it in the freezer to use when you want them during the upcoming year.

KITCHEN &
PANTRY BASICS

KITCHEN ORGANIZATION:

Once you toss the wrapping paper, you discover shiny new appliances, dishes, and glassware. Add the groceries and you may feel chaos. Where should you put everything?

It is time to create the perfect pantry and organize the kitchen. No, it need not be the double-doored, multishelved closet featured in the magazines, but your studio apartment has even more need for a well-organized pantry and kitchen than those larger, glamorous kitchens. How can you ever get organized?

Take a minute and plan your routine. Walk around and pretend you are simmering soup, tossing salad, or baking cookies. Think about the utensils, pans, or equipment you might use, and then plan how to take the fewest steps to reach them. Can you possibly stand in one spot and reach everything you need?

Group items you will typically use together in one spots. The mixer, bowls, and measuring cups become the baking center. Place cutting boards close to knives and mugs by the coffee maker or teapot.

Store those items you use daily in the most convenient spots, and those that you use infrequently in more out-of-the-way spots. If you cannot start your day without a smoothie, keep the blender handy, but if you think of using the blender just for icy drinks when your friends are gathering, you can store it farther back.

Stash the pot holders and tools you need to grab quickly by the stove. Cooking spoons, pancake turners, whisks, tongs, and other tools must be ready when you need them and it is vital to keep the pot holders near the stove.

Let safety rule. Keep knives in a block and not loose in a drawer. If counter space doesn't allow for the knife block, there are many other safe options available, such as a wall-mounted magnetic knife strip or holder or a knife holder that fits into a drawer. If an appliance is too heavy to lift safely, do not place it up high, and take care when storing sharp appliance blades.

Prep. Cook. Serve and enjoy. Store. Repeat. Before starting any recipe, assemble all of the tools and equipment you will need to execute the recipe. Wash, trim, and chop produce. Measure all ingredients. Preheat the oven. Select pans and grease or line them with parchment paper if it is required. These steps will make the cooking go more smoothly. Then, serve dinner attractively and savor every bite—yes, use those pretty serving bowls and placemats. Then, after dining, clean it up and return each ingredient and utensil to its spot, ready for next time. You will find it makes the cooking process quicker, easier, and much less stressful. This is especially true now that there are two of you in the kitchen. You do not want to find out midway through the recipe that your sweetie used the last of the olive oil or vinegar and failed to mention it (or failed to purchase a new bottle), and you won't have to go on a mad race trying to locate the tongs while the meat in the skillet burns.

Communicating about everyday tasks such as cooking makes everything run more smoothly. Mount a whiteboard, chalkboard, or bulletin board in the kitchen or behind a closet or pantry door. Write notes to each other about what's for dinner and keep a running grocery list. Yes, handwritten notes are old-fashioned, and you might think that a tablet or computer is the way to go, and that is fine, as long as you both can access the list quickly. But leaving a mobile device out in the car or in your backpack, or setting it anywhere you can't find it instantly, will not help you keep that list!

PANTRY ORGANIZATION:

An organized pantry makes cooking less stressful and saves money. So just what is a pantry? It is the room, closet, cabinet, or shelf where the food, utensils, and dishes are kept. So every kitchen has a pantry, whether you have a strategy or not. Plan and organize your storage and you will have a treasure chest; ignore what you stuff in the kitchen cabinet and let partially used boxes or bags of food collect naturally, and you will have a costly mess of this and that.

Where do you begin? Think about the kinds of menus you will serve and use them as a guide.

Keep like items together in zones. Baking powder, baking soda, flour, and sugar become a baking zone. Canned foods can be grouped together in one zone—with all of the canned fruit, tomatoes, and beans in one area or everything you need for chili (chili powder, tomatoes, beans, etc.) in its own zone if that is a specialty of yours. Likewise, if Asian-inspired dishes are a specialty for one of you and Italian the specialty of another, you might want to assemble separate zones with all you need to create those tantalizing meals.

Make items easy to find. Use clear containers so you can spot the contents as well as estimate the volume at a glance. Use lazy Susans or cabinet bleachers so items are easy to spot.

Label everything. Yes, many foods today are date coded (see page 175), but keep a permanent marker nearby to label items with the date when you opened them.

Keep foods tightly sealed; food in open containers will not stay fresh. Just like bags or boxes of chips or crackers, partially used boxes of cereal or pancake mix stay fresher if tightly sealed in a storage container.

Where to put it? Bins that keep potatoes and onions dry and cool are ideal. Place the bins on the floor, or in a cool, dark spot, but store them in separate bins—if they are stored together, natural gases will intermingle and cause the potatoes to spoil more quickly. Bread is best stored at room temperature, as bread stored in a refrigerator will stale. Store spices in individual airtight containers, away from heat and light—not over the stove. Check them periodically to make sure the spices are still fresh (contrary to popular belief, they don't have an unlimited shelf life, at least not flavorwise).

Rotate items in the pantry so you always operate on a first in, first out method. Place recently purchased items in the back and move older ones to the front for easy use.

The pantry is not just storage for leftovers—look at it as a cache of fantastic future dinners. Keep a variety of flavor additions handy, for they are the quick fix or vibrant flavor additions that transform everyday meals into spectacular dishes!

Think of the refrigerator and freezer as part of your pantry. Check product labels to see if there are recommendations regarding storage. Open bottles of salad dressings, marinades, and sauces usually must be refrigerated. If you're unsure if they need to be refrigerated, visit the manufacturer's website for recommendations.

SHOPPING LIST

BAKING NECESSITIES
- [ ] All-purpose flour
- [ ] Baking powder
- [ ] Baking soda
- [ ] Brown sugar
- [ ] Confectioners' powdered sugar
- [ ] Cornstarch
- [ ] Sugar
- [ ] Vanilla extract

CANNED, JARRED & DRIED
- [ ] Artichokes
- [ ] Beans
- [ ] Broth (low-sodium beef, chicken, vegetable)
- [ ] Chipotle peppers in adobo sauce
- [ ] Dried cranberries
- [ ] Dry bread crumbs
- [ ] Panko bread crumbs
- [ ] Roasted red peppers
- [ ] Sun-dried tomatoes
- [ ] Tomatoes (diced, crushed, sauce, paste)

DAIRY
- [ ] Butter
- [ ] Cheese (chunks, sliced, shredded)
- [ ] Milk
- [ ] Sour cream
- [ ] Yogurt (regular, Greek)

FAVORITES
- [ ] Chocolate-hazelnut spread
- [ ] Honey
- [ ] Jam and jelly
- [ ] Peanut butter

FRESH PRODUCE
- [ ] Garlic
- [ ] Ginger
- [ ] Lemons
- [ ] Limes
- [ ] Onions
- [ ] Potatoes
- [ ] Shallots

NUTS
- [ ] Almonds
- [ ] Pecans
- [ ] Pine nuts
- [ ] Walnuts

OILS & VEGETABLE SHORTENING
- [ ] Canola or vegetable oil
- [ ] Nonstick spray
- [ ] Olive oil
- [ ] Sesame oil
- [ ] Vegetable shortening

RICE & PASTA
- [ ] Brown rice
- [ ] Long-grain rice
- [ ] Penne or macaroni
- [ ] Spaghetti

SAUCES & FLAVOR BOOSTS
- [ ] Barbecue sauce
- [ ] Dijon mustard
- [ ] Ketchup
- [ ] Marinara or pasta sauce
- [ ] Mayonnaise
- [ ] Mirin
- [ ] Miso
- [ ] Salsa
- [ ] Salsa verde
- [ ] Soy sauce

- [ ] Sriracha or other hot sauce
- [ ] Worcestershire sauce

SPICES & SEASONINGS
- [ ] Basil (dried)
- [ ] Cayenne pepper
- [ ] Chili powder
- [ ] Cinnamon (ground, sticks)
- [ ] Cumin (ground)
- [ ] Garlic (powdered, minced dried)
- [ ] Italian seasoning
- [ ] Mustard (powdered)
- [ ] Oregano (dried)
- [ ] Paprika
- [ ] Pepper, black (ground, whole peppercorns)
- [ ] Red pepper flakes
- [ ] Salt
- [ ] Thyme leaves (dried)

VINEGAR
- [ ] Apple cider vinegar
- [ ] Balsamic vinegar
- [ ] Red wine vinegar
- [ ] Rice vinegar
- [ ] White wine vinegar

STORAGE & PAPER SUPPLIES
- [ ] Aluminum foil (regular and nonstick/release foil)
- [ ] Parchment paper
- [ ] Plastic wrap
- [ ] Storage containers with tight-fitting lids
- [ ] Zip-top food storage bags (gallon-size)
- [ ] Zip-top freezer bags

TIPS FOR SAVVY COOKING:

These are tips and tricks our years of cooking have taught us. Oh, we wish we had known all of these things when we started cooking! We thought we would save you from struggling the way we did in the beginning.

OLIVE OIL: There is a wide array of domestic and imported olive oils available, and you need not purchase the most expensive. Those labeled *cold pressed* are preferred, as the oil is extracted by pressure and not with chemicals. Extra-virgin olive oil is a fine oil that comes from the first pressing so it is fruity and more expensive. It is especially good for salad dressings or drizzling on Italian bread—times when the fruity flavor will be appreciated. Virgin olive oil is less expensive and is just slightly more acidic so it is a good choice, especially if used in cooking. "Light" olive oil is confusing, as it has the same amount of fat and number of calories—the "light" actually refers to the oil being highly filtered and lighter in color and body than extra-virgin or virgin olive oil. Olive oil breaks down at higher temperatures so if you sauté with it, do not use a high heat.

FLOUR: To measure any kind of flour (all-purpose or whole-grain), spoon the flour out of the flour canister and into the cup, then level it off with the flat edge of a table knife. This is known as the spoon-and-sweep method. Do not dip the measuring cup into the flour canister, nor shake the cup to level it off. Store whole-grain flour, tightly sealed, in the refrigerator for up to 6 months or in the freezer for up to 1 year.

BROWN SUGAR: Brown sugar is labeled *dark* or *light* and you can use them interchangeably. The dark brown version has a more intense molasses flavor and is popular in Southern cooking. We find you often use the one you grew up with or the type that is most familiar to you—so Roxanne chooses dark and Kathy chooses light. Brown sugar is always measured "packed" to ensure that any pockets of air have been pressed out of the sugar (since brown sugar is slightly moist, it doesn't automatically settle like regular granulated sugar does). Spoon it into the measuring cup and pack it lightly; it should hold its shape when turned out into the bowl.

SALT: Today salt comes in a variety of colors, origins, and textures. Kosher salt can be used for all cooking because it dissolves quickly. Sea salt is crystalline in shape and is ideal to sprinkle on cooked foods as a finishing touch. Fleur de sel, a sea salt from France (the name of which translates to "flower of the sea"), is a delicately flavored specialty salt and due to its cost, it is a special-occasion salt that should be sprinkled over food just before eating. Table salt is finely ground and is available with and without the addition of iodine, a necessary nutrient. It is fun to experiment with the varieties available. We tend to use kosher salt for savory cooking and table salt for baking cakes and cookies.

BUTTER: We prefer unsalted (sometimes labeled "sweet") butter for cooking, and it is the butter used for all of the recipes in this book. We do not recommend using margarine. When cooking, it is difficult to substitute "light" or butter spreads as they have a higher moisture content than regular butter. Using lighter or diet varieties will affect the texture and flavor of the baked good or dish. Purchase butter when it's on sale, then store it in the freezer for up to 9 months.

CHEESE: Chunks of cheese that you slice or shred as you need them will provide the freshest, best flavor. However, the grocery aisles are packed with every variety of chunk, shred, or slice imaginable, and those that are sliced or shredded offer convenience. In this book, if we list shredded cheese, you may shred it yourself using a box grater or a food processor, or turn to the packaged variety. Please, avoid using (or at least don't tell us if you do) a can of grated Parmesan cheese or a block of pasteurized cheese spread. Those cheeses labeled "reduced fat" may not melt as smoothly or taste as rich as the full-fat variety, and the quality and melted texture vary by brand. If you want to use the lower fat varieties, experiment with different brands to find the best.

HERBS, SEASONINGS & FLAVOR BOOSTS:

Hidden behind those pantry doors are all kinds of flavor boosts for every dish.

Your memory of Grandma's cooking may get your taste buds excited, and yet, while comforting and good, all too often old-fashioned cooking means dishes were mildly seasoned. Today our taste buds beg for more intensely flavored dishes, and bold is the name of the game. You are used to restaurant meals and international cuisines and that means your taste buds are attuned to spices, herbs, and flavor boosts never imagined a few years ago. Your pantry becomes a spicy cache of flavor.

FRESH AND DRIED HERBS:

Herbs and spices will add the flavor you are seeking.

FRESH:

» For fresh herbs, always select those with bright colors that show no signs of wilting. Keep herbs refrigerated in a damp paper towel sealed in a zip-top bag, or place the stems of a bouquet of herbs in a glass of water and cover with a plastic bag. Snip off the leaves you need for a dish. If mincing fresh herbs for a recipe, place the leaves on the cutting board and cut, using a rocking motion, with a sharp chef's knife, or place the herbs in a cup or small bowl, then use the tip of kitchen scissors to finely snip them.

» Fresh herbs add a great flavor punch, but heat and long cooking may fade their flavor. Always taste and add additional fresh herbs during the last few minutes of cooking. This is especially true in a slow cooker (see page 184).

DRIED:

» Bottles of dried herbs, spices, and seasoning blends are convenient and are readily available when fresh isn't possible. You will also find tasty blends and combinations you never dreamed possible! To extract the most flavor from dried herbs, crumble them in your hands just before adding them to the dish.

» Be sure to remove bay leaves just before serving so no one chokes on them.

» Age, light, and heat are the enemies of dried herbs and spices in those little bottles. Store herbs and spices in a cool, dark place, away from heat. That means not in the cabinet or shelf over the stove or refrigerator. Most professionals recommend keeping open bottles of herbs or seasonings for just 6 months to a year. Yes, they are expensive and it is tempting to keep them longer, but you want to avoid hoarding open bottles of spices until the flavor diminishes and they stale. Buy small bottles that you can use up. You might visit a store that sells bulk spices and buy just what you need. Or, share half with your coworker or neighbor. If the bottle is not date-coded, use a marker to write the date when you opened it.

» If you begin to use an old, open bottle of dried herbs and it has no aroma—or you cannot identify if it is cinnamon or chili powder based on the aroma—why are you using it? It will add no flavor, or if it does add flavor, it may impart an off or stale flavor to the dish you are cooking.

» Add herbs, spices, salts, and seasonings conservatively at first, then add more as needed toward the end of cooking. This is just prudent as you can always add seasonings,
but it is difficult to remove one that is "too much." Generally substitute 1 teaspoon of
dried leaf herbs for 1 tablespoon of minced fresh herbs.

» Never underestimate salt and pepper. Salt not only adds flavor, it balances, blends,
and brightens the other seasonings. Pepper may add the perfect little kick, especially
if you freshly grind the pepper.

QUICK SEASONINGS FOR MEAT:

» **DRY RUBS:** Dry rubs are seasoning blends that are rubbed onto the surface of the meat prior to cooking. Dry rubs that contain ground chiles
(such as chili powder) and sugar should be used on quick-cooking
meats as chiles and sugar brown quickly and can cause overbrowning
if cooked too long.

These simple herb blends may add just the flavor you are seeking—
or are a starting point to create your own signature blend:

» **TUSCAN:** Blend together minced garlic or garlic powder with dried basil
leaves, oregano leaves, and rosemary. Season with salt and pepper.

» **MEXICAN:** Begin with chili powder and stir in ground cumin and dried
oregano leaves. Do not forget the salt and pepper. Add a bit of
cayenne if you enjoy heat.

» **ASIAN:** Season the meat with peeled, minced fresh ginger, garlic, red
pepper flakes, salt, and pepper.

» If selecting a seasoning blend, read the label. You may discover the blend lists salt first (which means it is the ingredient in the largest volume) followed by a small amount of herbs as well as preservatives or chemicals. Other blends are a wonderful combination of herbs or seasonings you might not already own and are worth the money.

» If you enjoy curries or highly spiced Mexican foods it is great to stock up on chiles, curry powder, or cumin. If not, don't avoid them, but when you do try a new recipe, buy the smallest container you can find or check out the bulk items aisle and purchase just the amount you need to use.

MARINATING 101:

Marinate beef, chicken, or pork in a simple marinade to add flavor and tenderize the meat. Most marinades are made of oil; an acid such as lemon juice, wine, or vinegar; salt and pepper; and often additional flavor boosts, such as herbs, soy sauce, mustard, or Worcestershire sauce.

With a well-stocked pantry, marinades go together quickly so there is no need to turn to bottled marinades. Plus, when making your own, it is very easy to adjust the flavor to your preference, reduce the sodium level, and avoid additives.

TO MARINATE:

» Place the meat in a zip-top bag (or in a glass dish) and add the marinade; seal the bag (or cover the dish). Marinate the meat in the refrigerator for the time indicated by the recipe. Chicken and fish will take on the flavor in just minutes, while less tender cuts of beef may marinate several hours or overnight.

» Drain and discard the marinade.

» Pat the meat dry with a paper towel and cook.

FLAVOR BOOSTS:

DRESS UP MAYONNAISE

For any sandwich, panini, grilled meat, or salad, transform mayonnaise into something special. Blend any one of the following into mayonnaise:

» Minced scallions or chives

» Minced fresh garlic

» Lemon juice, grated lemon zest, and a few grinds of pepper

» Minced fresh garlic and finely minced fresh basil

» Chopped canned artichoke hearts, drained, and shredded Parmesan cheese

FLAVOR A PANCAKE OR WAFFLE MIX

Stir any one of these favorites into the batter before baking:

» Mini chocolate chips

» Chopped, toasted nuts

» Crisp, crumbled bacon

» Ground cinnamon, nutmeg, or ginger

» Vanilla, maple, or lemon extract

OATMEAL FLAVOR BOOSTS

Top that bowl of oatmeal with:

» Chopped, toasted nuts

» Fresh blueberries, sliced strawberries or bananas, or any favorite fresh fruit

» Dried cranberries, blueberries, cherries, or raisins, or dried, chopped apricots, apples, or other dried fruits

» Flavored low-fat yogurt

» Ground cinnamon, nutmeg, or ginger

RAISE THE BAR ON RICE

» Replace equal portions of the water with broth, tomato juice, diced tomatoes, or white wine.

» Stir in dried Italian seasoning or dried basil, oregano, thyme, or other dried herb leaves.

» Sauté chopped onion, garlic, shallot, red or green bell pepper, sliced mushrooms, celery, or minced carrots until tender, then add the rice and liquids according to the package directions.

GROCERY SHOPPING SAVVY:

Grocery success begins at home. The plans you make take a few minutes but save lots of time, money, and stress in the end. Remember, there are two of you, so talk everything over—including the budget, the meal expectations and what you will serve, who will cook, and even your food quirks, diet, and guilty pleasures. Don't let "little" differences, such as who will cook, how healthy to make the meal, or how much to spend, escalate into your own version of *Chopped* or *Kitchen Wars*.

Set a budget. What is a realistic amount that your household income will allow for food? What kinds of meals and groceries do you prefer? Do you enjoy buying top-quality, gourmet items and accompanying the meals with wine? Or, would you prefer simpler, less expensive meals? Plan the budget together and experiment to see if it is realistic. Compromise on your goal and make a pact to stick to it. It is not to say you can't ever splurge, but that is a once-in-a-while treat, not a weekly oops. If you enjoy eating out, be sure to remember that restaurant meals are costly and add that amount to your weekly food budget.

Planning for two servings often takes more careful preparation than cooking for a larger family. Cooking larger recipes may provide more leftovers than you wish to have. Also, many items are packaged for families so using it up prior to spoilage may be a problem. For example, if you two are not avid bread eaters, buy a loaf and freeze some for later use. While a gallon of milk may be a great buy, it is a waste of money if it spoils prior to use.

Plan your meals—not just for tonight, but for several meals. What is the main dish and key side dish? Posting it allows you both to know, so whoever comes home first can start the meal. More important, if you shop with those menus in mind, you can be sure to purchase what you need. It is also easier to use up partial ingredients. For example, if you used chicken broth in a sauce you can plan to use the broth in the soup a few days later.

Check your staples and pantry. Keep your pantry organized so you can quickly scan and see what you have or what you need. Mount a whiteboard, chalkboard, bulletin board or notepad inside a cabinet so you can get in the habit of making a grocery list and writing down items as you need them. Add staples to the list as you get toward the bottom of the box so you can replace it. (Do you want to keep that list electronically? Go for it, but be sure the device is always close by for if you must hunt for it you won't keep the list up-to-date. A whiteboard on the inside on the cabinet door is always in the same place and always handy.)

Check the ads, coupons, and online specials before leaving for the store. You will discover if chicken breasts are on sale and therefore worthy of stocking up on, or if seasonal fruits or a specific meat cut is on sale and is one you would like to include in the menu plan for the week.

Clip coupons, organize your stash, and use them. If your store has a customer reward program, use it and maximize your savings. Frequently, you can use a manufacturer's coupon or online coupon in combination with a reward program for maximum savings. Check out couponing websites for couponing classes, tips, and guides, and if someone teaches a class or offers a webinar, take it—you will learn many great ideas.

Buy in season or visit farmers' markets. You will find you eat healthier, will enjoy the freshest produce available, and may discover new varieties of old favorites. Produce that is in season is plentiful and less expensive. Talk to the farmers and you will discover it is easy to choose items that are organic or grown without chemicals or pesticides.

Make a list and stick to it. Do not shop when you are hungry. You will be tempted to add snacks or spur-of-the-moment purchases.

While some larger packages cost less per serving, it is not guaranteed. Evaluate the cost per serving. If storage space is at a premium, they may not be a great buy for you no matter what the price might be. Many stores post the cost per ounce on a shelf tag, so compare and choose the best one for you. Also, if you are trying a new recipe or learning to cook a new cuisine, avoid the larger packages until you hone your skill and know you enjoy that recipe.

Stock up on sale items, especially if it is an item you purchase frequently or use regularly when cooking. If you open a new jar of marinara every 2 to 3 weeks, buying several extra ones when they are on sale is wise. However, if a bottle of oil or soy sauce lasts you a year, do not buy several bottles just because they are on sale.

Compare brands and be flexible. If you are brand specific, admit it, especially so your spouse knows you will not even try an alternate brand of coffee or peanut butter. For many items, however, you will find that brands are similar and store brands offer substantial savings over name brands.

Compromise and plan together. Since there are two of you in the kitchen, you might alternate cooking tasks. Maybe you each pick a couple of menus and write the needed items on the grocery list. If one of you has special allergies or dietary needs, planning becomes even more important.

Minimize surprises that affect your budget. For example, some couples are surprised to learn how much money goes toward groceries. If your grocery budget includes paper goods or cleaning supplies, that is fine, but be aware of it. If you use cash at the farmers' market but a debit card at the grocery store, be sure to keep track of the total you spent on the groceries. Dinners out or last-minute guests are fun, but do not let the costs creep up unexpectedly if you are trying to stick to a budget or trim expenditures.

The healthiest and often cheapest foods are around the perimeter of the store. This is where foods that are less processed reside—the fresh produce, meats, dairy, etc. To avoid temptation, especially when trying to make healthy purchases and save money, avoid those center aisles stacked with candy, chips, and soda.

DATE CODES:

While convenient, dates codes are not legally required (except on formula and baby foods) and may actually cause a bit of confusion. There are no set standards and each manufacturer sets its own dates regarding quality. The wording is often tricky. Read the label carefully and if you have questions about the storage time of a particular food, visit the producer's or food company's website.

There is no need to throw out everything that is past the stamped date. Of course, if the food has developed an off odor or appearance, throw it out without question. (It is always better to be safe than sorry.) However, many items may still be wholesome and safe to eat—even if the quality has begun to fade.

» **SELL-BY DATE:** Tells the store how long to display the product for sale. Purchase the item before that date for the best quality. (Be sure to check carefully at the store and if necessary, hunt for the freshest. Do not be embarrassed to dig to the back of the display to find the freshest.)

» **BEST IF USED BY:** A recommendation for the best flavor or quality. It is not a safety date.

» **USE-BY DATE:** The last date recommended for peak quality.

Do you want to add convenience? Generally, items that are in a more natural state cost less than items where one or more preparation steps have been done for you. For example, lettuce in heads or bunches cost less than salad mixes, and whole carrots cost less than trimmed baby carrots. Ground beef costs less than premade beef patties. Neither is wrong and either can fit into a budget—just make an informed decision.

Check out salad bars, olive bars, and delis. While the price per pound of prepared foods is more than buying the whole item, you may find there is so much less waste that it becomes a sound purchase for you. For example, if you want to use just three or four olives, buying that amount and not a whole can is wise. Likewise, a few broccoli florets from the salad bar may be wise if you are just using it in one stir-fry dish and do not have plans to use the whole bunch. It also may be a wise purchase if the convenience helps you to get a quick meal on the table on a busy evening so you can avoid eating out.

Stay out of the store on non-shopping days. Shopping every day adds to the cost and zaps your time. If you shop daily, it sounds easy, but realistically, you will spend about 30 minutes, and suddenly you have wasted a couple of hours that week on groceries.

Keep the kitchen savvy going and store your purchases correctly when you get home. Don't just dump everything out of the bag; put things where they belong, placing newer items behind the open, older items in your pantry and following the guidelines below for other items.

PRODUCE: Generally, wash produce when you get home. (Notable exceptions are mushrooms, berries, potatoes, and onions—these items should be washed just prior to using them.) Wash lettuce and greens and pack them between paper towels in sealed zip-top bags. Be sure to wash fruits, including citrus, well. Scrub cantaloupes and melons with a vegetable brush under running water.

MEAT: Refrigerate meat quickly after shopping. Plan to use ground beef or chicken in 1 or 2 days, or freeze for use in the weeks to come. Beef or pork steaks or roasts may be kept in the refrigerator for 3 to 5 days, or frozen for later use. While it looks tight, the plastic wrapping around the meat package used by typical grocery stores is not freezer-ready, and if you freeze the meat without additional wrapping, the meat will dry out. Slip the package into a freezer bag, seal it tightly, label, and freeze. Separate larger packages of meat into usable sizes—packing one or two chicken pieces together, making ½-pound packages of ground beef, or separating other meats into sizes typical of what you might use. If you plan to freeze bacon, separate every two or three slices with parchment or waxed paper, then it seal all in a freezer bag. Once frozen, you can separate them and use just a slice or two as needed. Thaw meats, still tightly wrapped, in the refrigerator.

SMALL APPLIANCE 101:

The first step toward becoming an appliance pro is to use that shiny new equipment from your registry, and to keep using it. Appliances can make kitchen tasks easier and quicker. Unpack them, become familiar with them, and use them.

Keep them handy. When planning where to store appliances, try to select a convenient spot. Place those you plan to use daily, such as the coffee maker, toaster, or that blender you want to use for your daily smoothie, right where you can reach them. If waffles might be a Saturday morning treat once a month, maybe the back of the cabinet is a good spot for the waffle maker.

Read the booklet or information packed with the appliance, or visit the manufacturer's website. You will discover all kinds of priceless information. You will find tips on how to use the appliance safely and efficiently, how to clean it, and even how to use the appliance in fun and unexpected ways. Always use the appliance as it was intended; if you try to use it in a way other than as it was intended, you are courting danger.

Write the date you received the appliance on the outside of the use and care information and keep it. Slip the information leaflets into plastic sleeves and keep them all in a 3-ring notebook, or scan the information and make an electronic file for easy reference.

BLENDER:

Blenders vary from basic blenders, which are ideal for sauces and drinks, to professional-quality blenders that are quite powerful—some of these models can grind grains, heat soup, and make frozen desserts. Not all blenders will perform in the same way, so if you are in doubt, check on the manufacturer's website to confirm the kind of blender you have.

BLENDER TIPS:

» Use short, quick pulses for more even chopping and blending.

» Blending is quick. Do not overdo it.

» Stop the motor and scrape down the sides of the blender jar with a rubber spatula as needed to promote even blending.

» Do not overfill the container. Most are marked with a "max fill" line. Work in batches, if necessary.

» Place the lid on the blender, and *then* turn it on. It is always wise to hold the lid in place while blending—better safe than sorry. Turn off the blender and allow it to come to a stop, then remove the lid and scrape the container or pour the contents out. The blades are quite sharp; do not place your hand into the blender jar.

» The lids on most blenders have a removable center. It is great to remove that center when drizzling in oil when making a salad dressing or pesto. It is necessary to remove the center of the lid to provide a vent if you blend a hot liquid, such as hot soup, so that any steam can safely escape. If you do not vent the lid, you need to let the liquid cool before blending.

GREAT USES:

» Blending drinks—milkshakes, smoothies, cocktails, and fitness drinks
» Blending sauces (especially hollandaise sauce), salad dressings (including mayonnaise), peanut or other nut butters, salsas, and dips
» Making purees for sauces or soups
» Mixing pancake batter or instant puddings
» Chopping small amounts of nuts, herbs, or bread or cracker crumbs

Not good for:

» Whipping cream or egg whites
» Grinding raw meat
» Mashing potatoes

» Start on a low speed, especially if blending a hot liquid, then increase to a higher speed.

» Most blenders will not chop ice unless there is liquid. Add juice, milk, or cocktail ingredients along with the ice and blend until it has a slushy consistency.

» Liquids help the blender to chop hard foods, such as carrots, cabbage, or other vegetables. Add some liquid (water is great) before adding the hard foods to chop. Cut the food into even 1-inch pieces and add the pieces to the blender jar. Place the lid on the blender, then chop, using quick pulses. Pour into a fine strainer to strain out the vegetables. Discard the water or use it for soups.

IMMERSION BLENDER:

What is an immersion blender and when do you use it? Immersion blenders are also called "stick blenders" or "wand blenders" and they look like a sharp, swirling blender blade on the end of a stick or handle. They are quite handy, but can be dangerous. An immersion blender does many of the same things as a countertop blender. You move the immersion blender to the food, placing it into the pot of cooked vegetables, for example, or down into the tall milk shake glass, instead of spooning the food into the deep blender jar as when using a countertop blender. An immersion blender is especially convenient to use when blending small amounts of salad dressing or sauce, or one drink, milk shake, or smoothie in a glass. It is also a wonderful tool to use when pureeing a soup; you can immerse the immersion blender in the pot of soup or cooked vegetables directly instead of transferring it to a countertop blender. Always use caution as the spinning blade at the base of the immersion blender is very sharp. For safety and to avoid splatters, be sure to immerse the immersion blender head deeply in the food prior to turning the blender on and turn it off before lifting it out of the food. A deep bowl will minimize any possibility of splatters. Never use your fingers to dislodge a piece of food or clean off the blade. Unplug the immersion blender before disassembling or removing the blades.

FOOD PROCESSOR:

From a mini-chopper to a large, almost industrial size, food processors come in a variety of sizes to fit your needs.

GREAT USES:

» Chopping produce or meat

» Slicing or shredding

» Mixing

» Kneading

» Preparing salsas, dips, spreads, and pestos

Not good for:

» Mashing or whipping potatoes

» Beating egg whites

» Blending liquids (if overfilled, it will leak)

FOOD PROCESSOR TIPS:

» All tasks are quick. Use short pulses to blend or process. Do not overprocess—it can happen quickly. For the most even slicing, stand food evenly in the feed tube and use steady, even pressure.

» Cut the food into even pieces that fit comfortably through the feed tube.

» Do not overload the bowl. It is always better to chop in smaller batches.

» Check the manufacturer's website for tips regarding cheese, as there are so many types of cheese and various models have different levels of power available. Many cheeses shred best when chilled. To grate hard cheese such as Parmesan, allow the cheese to come to room temperature, cut it into cubes, and process using the metal blade. Do not attempt to slice Parmesan or soft cheeses such as mozzarella.

» Making pastry in a food processor is quick and effortless. Be sure not to overprocess. Stop the motor just as the dough comes together to form a ball around the blade.

» If one recipe has several steps, begin with the driest ingredients to chop, grate, or blend, remove the food, then go right on to blend or mix a moist step. This order makes the tasks, and the cleanup, go more quickly and easily.

» Food processors are sold by the size of their work bowls, listed in cups of dry ingredients. However, this is a little confusing when it comes to liquids. Generally, if processing liquids, fill the processor bowl only about half full to avoid leaks. Also, if mixing heavy dough or kneading bread, you should follow the manufacturer's recommendation for the number of cups of flour that can be used in one recipe.

SLOW COOKER:

Slow cookers are now available from small 1-quart units to large 6- or 7-quart units, or even as multiple vessels in one appliance or vessels that hook together to operate as one. Slow cookers can be round or oval. Many families find they use two or more different slow cookers—smaller ones for dips and larger ones for chili when tailgating.

GREAT USES:

» Soups, stews, chilies, and sauces

» Roasting less-tender cuts of meat due to long, slow simmering

Not good for:

» Boiling pasta

» Cooking with milk, sour cream, or cheese (unless added toward the end of the cooking time)

SLOW COOKER TIPS:

» Cook, with the cover on, for the time recommended or until the food is done and tender. Do not lift the cover to peek or stir.

» You will have more liquid at the end of the cooking than what you began. If you adapt a recipe to the slow cooker, reduce the amount of liquid used in the recipe.

» Use dry minced garlic to impart a true garlic flavor when slow cooking. The flavor of fresh herbs, fresh garlic, and even many dried herbs will fade while slow cooking. If you wish to use fresh herbs, add them at the end of cooking. We always recommend that you taste the dish just before serving and add additional seasonings as desired. If using dried herbs, select dried leaf seasonings instead of the ground varieties. Be sure the dried herbs are not old or stale; stale herbs offer very little flavor and, worse, can impart a bitter flavor, especially when slow cooking.

» Generally, 1 hour on high equals about 2 hours on low. You can use this tip to adjust the cooking time to fit the time you have.

» Many slow cookers now have removable stoneware vessels. You can fill the stoneware vessel with the recipe ingredients the night before, cover it, and place it in the refrigerator. In the morning, all you need to do is place the stoneware vessel in the heating base, cover it, and turn the slow cooker on, and you're out the door.

STAND MIXER:

Heavy-duty stand mixers are investments and generally last for many years.

STAND MIXER TIPS:

» Insert or remove the mixing attachments (such as the dough hook, whisk, or paddle) with the mixer unplugged.

» Many mixers have a variety of attachments available. You can find attachments to prepare pasta, grind meats or grains, shred or slice vegetables or fruits, juice citrus fruits, or make ice cream. Check with the manufacturer of your mixer to see what attachments are available, and then evaluate carefully to determine if the attachment is one you would use.

GREAT USES:

» Creaming shortening or butter and sugar

» Beating egg whites, cream, and meringues

» Mixing dough for cookies and breads

» Kneading bread dough, especially with the dough hook available on many models

» Grinding meat (with a special attachment)

» Extruding or pressing pasta dough (with a special attachment)

Not good for:

» Very small volumes

» Why use a stand mixer versus a handheld mixer? If you are whipping a small amount of cream or just an egg white, a handheld mixer might be ideal. Handheld mixers are also powerful enough to prepare cake mixes and beat light batters. However, many models are not powerful enough to beat larger volumes of food, mix heavy cookie dough, or knead bread. If in doubt, review the use and care information on the manufacturer's website for a list of recommended foods and to find out which ones to avoid.

» Depending on the brand of the mixer and shape of the bowl and beater, some large mixers cannot adequately mix just a cup or two or whip one egg white. Mix or whip these smaller volumes using a handheld mixer.

MULTI GRILL:

With so many uses and just one appliance to store, the multi grill makes an ideal choice for many. This one cooking appliance comes with a variety of interchangeable grids so you can use it as a grill, griddle, panini press, or perhaps a waffle maker.

MULTI GRILL TIPS:

» Assemble the plates you wish to use for the cooking task before preheating.

» Set the temperature dial to the prescribed temperature for the task you will be performing. Preheat until the indicator light comes on.

» Cooking is quick. Check the cooking progress and cook until the food is fully cooked but not overcooked.

» The surfaces are very hot. Use caution.

» If your model came with a removable drip pan, be sure to have it correctly in place before cooking.

» Some models are available that do not have removable or interchangeable plates, but work great for a single use, such as grilling meats in a contact grill, making toasty panini, or baking waffles. Some couples may select one of these appliances if they do not anticipate using all of the functions (or plates) of a multi grill. If the plates are not removeable, unplug the unit, allow it to cool, then wipe the plates clean with a damp cloth.

GREAT USES:

» As a panini press for crisp, hot sandwiches

» As a griddle for pancakes, eggs, sandwiches, French toast, bacon, or sausages

» As an open grill or a closed contact grill for grilling meats, such as boneless chicken, steaks, burgers, or fish

Not good for:

» Deep-frying

» Bone-in chicken pieces

WAFFLE MAKER:

If you are a fan of waffles, be sure to add a waffle maker to your registry. You may also find your multi grill has waffle plates available as an accessory.

WAFFLE MAKER TIPS:

» If your waffle maker has removable plates, or if you're using waffle plates on a multi grill, assemble the plates and be sure they are correctly in place before preheating.

» Preheat until the indicator light comes on.

» The surfaces are very hot. Use caution.

» Ladle the batter into the center of the grid. Check the manufacturer's directions for an estimate regarding the volume needed to make a waffle and do not overfill the grid.

» Bake until the indicator light comes on and the steaming stops. If you open the waffle iron too early, the waffle will stick.

GREAT USES:

» Waffles for breakfast or brunch
» Waffles for lunch or dinner with chicken or other meat
» Sweet waffles or chocolate waffles for dessert
» Hash brown potatoes

Not good for:

» Grilling meats

ICE CREAM MAKER:

Tabletop-size ice cream makers that churn just a quart are ideal for couples, and newer models eliminate the messy salt and ice required for older versions.

ICE CREAM MAKER TIPS:

» New, tabletop ice cream freezers do not require salt.

» Put the freezer container in the freezer for at least 24 hours If you make ice cream frequently, store the container in your freezer.

» Look for the "max fill" line and do not overfill.

» The appliance is often automatic and may turn off when the ice cream is done, usually in 20 to 30 minutes.

GREAT USES:

» Ice cream

» Frozen yogurt

» Sherbets and sorbets

» Gelato

Not good for:

» Frozen drinks

CUTLERY:

What is the most important tool in a kitchen? Most cooks—home cooks and chefs alike—report emphatically that it is a sharp knife. It does not matter if you have two or three shiny new ones, or received that megablock with lots of polished, matching knives: A good knife is indispensible.

Old lore used to deter people from giving knives as gifts—and we hope your family and friends did not follow those tales. Once, if a friend gave a knife, it meant the friendship might be severed, so to be prudent a penny or other coin might be taped to the gift box so the recipient could quickly pay the giver for the gift. Surely, we have moved beyond this silliness, and you registered for—and received—the knives of your dreams.

If you did not register or receive those knives, shop carefully to select the best knives for your family. You will be using them daily for years to come and you will want to make a sound decision. Also, do not be swayed into thinking that you must buy a block with lots of knives. You can select a knife or two now, then add knives as time, and needs, change.

First, pick them up and see how they feel in your hands. Are they balanced? Does the fit feel right? Both of you need to test the feel and be sure it feels right, for both larger and smaller hands.

MATERIALS:

HIGH-CARBON STAINLESS STEEL: Especially popular for good knives, it combines the sharp edge of a carbon-steel blade with the rust and corrosion resistance of stainless steel. It is an ideal choice, but expensive.

CARBON STEEL: Long used for knives, it can be sharpened to a very sharp edge. The downside is that it stains and rusts easily.

STAINLESS STEEL: This once popular material is still occasionally found in less expensive knives. While pretty, stainless-steel knives are hard to sharpen.

CERAMIC: Now used for knives, ceramic makes a hard blade that does not corrode, and it can hold a sharp edge for a long time. However, is brittle, so if you drop a ceramic knife, the blade may crack.

Technology and manufacturing practices change, so if you find you are replacing a knife in years to come, do not just take the manufacturer's claims at face value. Read some current, nonbiased reviews so you can make an up-to-date, sound decision.

PARTS OF A KNIFE:

The tang is the portion of the blade that runs through the handle. Top-quality knives will have a tang that runs all the way through the knife.

The handle of a knife may be made of wood or plastic—or even be a continuation of the metal used in the blade. The material is more a matter of personal preference, but how you plan to care for the knives should also affect your choice. Test the grip and see how the handle feels.

CARE & CLEANING:

Avoid the dishwasher. Even if the marketing material says you can place it in the dishwasher, most food professionals will recommend against it for so many reasons. First, it is a matter of safety. Grabbing a knife from the dishwasher is dangerous, and typically someone gets cut. Second, the hot water and detergent dulls the knife and the sharp points can even pierce plastic coated shelves or edges in the dishwasher. In addition, if the knife has a wooden handle, the dishwasher dries it out. Wash knives separately in hot, soapy water, rinse, and dry.

Remember, there are two of you in the kitchen and if your sweetie is nice enough to wash the dishes, don't surprise him or her with sharp knives hidden in the soapy dishwater.

SHARPENING:

That metal rod in the knife block is called a steel and is used to sharpen your knives. It is essential, because if you use it correctly and regularly, it will help maintain the sharp edge on your blades. Hold the blade of the knife at a 20 degree angle to the steel and lightly glide the knife over the steel three or four times. Wash the knife and you are good to go. Do not get crazy and overdo it—you don't have to use the steel after every cut—but make a regular habit of it and your knives will maintain sharp edges longer. Now, where do you store them?

STORAGE:

Please do not throw knives loose in a drawer—one of you will be cut while fishing for a knife. If you do not have a block or if the block will not fit in a tiny kitchen, there are many other safe options available, such as a magnetic knife strip or a knife holder that fits into a drawer. There are also plastic sleeves that slip over the blades. Evaluate your space and let safety be your guide.

POPULAR KNIVES:

Sure, that big megablock is great. However, if you are selecting a few top-quality knives, these are the most popular ones.

FRENCH OR CHEF'S KNIFE: An all-purpose knife 6 to 10 inches long

PARING KNIFE: A smaller knife for fine, detailed work or peeling

BREAD KNIFE: A long knife with a serrated edge that makes it easier to slice bread and soft foods like tomatoes

SLICING OR CARVING KNIFE: A longer, thinner knife for slicing meats

ELECTRIC KNIVES:

Did you receive an electric knife? Odds are you might have one for it is among the most popular presents in the small appliance category. An electric knife is ideal for slicing most meats, from roasts to chicken, turkey, brisket, or ham, and it is handy for lots of other foods. An electric knife:

» Cuts through the crust of bread—artisan, crusty loaves, or freshly baked loaves.

» Slices angel food cake without mashing.

» Slices melon, pineapple, and squash that have tough outer rinds.

» Is *not* for slicing through bones.

TO USE AN ELECTRIC KNIFE:

Unplug the knife and be sure to lock any safety latches before inserting the blades. Once the blades are securely in place, plug it in, then press the on switch. There is no need to exert pressure—let the motor and vibrating knife blades do the work. Once you are finished slicing, unplug the knife and lock the safety latches before removing the blades.

KNIFE SAVVY:

» Hold the knife securely between your thumb and index finger. Use your opposite hand to hold the food and guide the knife. Curl your fingertips on the guiding hand out of the way and the side of the knife blade can slide safely against your knuckles.

» Sharper, well-cared-for knives that are used correctly are safer, and you do not want to join the throngs of cooks who lament that a dull knife slipped and nicked a finger.

» Use the center of the blade for most cutting and chopping.

» Use the tip when cutting details or fine, thin slices. Use the base or heel of the knife when cutting through heavy, hard foods.

CUTLERY ADDITIONS:

KITCHEN SCISSORS OR SHEARS: You will use this indispensable tool daily. Far beyond snipping a bag open, scissors make quick work of mincing herbs, cutting raw or crisp cooked bacon, dicing dried apricots or other dried fruits, or even slicing a pizza instead of using a pizza cutter. Don't use your office scissors for cooking tasks; they need to be separate tools.

PIZZA CUTTER: This great tool is sharp, so store it carefully but keep it handy for slicing pizza, cutting the crusts off slices of bread, cutting wedges from tortillas, and so many other uses.

POULTRY SHEARS: While you will find this tool beneficial if you attempt to cut up a whole chicken, you will also turn to it when trimming fat from chicken breasts or cutting chicken quarters into smaller pieces. These sturdy shears are also great for cutting through the

CUTTING TERMINOLOGY:

» **DICE:** cut into tiny, even cubes, $1/8$ to $1/4$ inch

» **CHOP:** cut into small or bite-size pieces

» **MINCE:** cut into very fine pieces

» **CUBE:** cut into even cubes, often of a specified size

No matter what knife you use, or what you are chopping, cutting, or slicing, keep the pieces even. The food will cook more evenly and look more attractive.

shells of lobster and other tough jobs. Quality reigns: Lightweight and inexpensive poultry shears may not be up to the task. Be sure the shears come apart for easy and thorough washing.

RASP-STYLE GRATER: Most often called Microplane graters (a common brand), rasp-style graters were once at home in the tool box, but are now a kitchen favorite. Use a rasp-style grater to zest citrus, grating off just the colored portion of the rind (the white pith beneath is bitter). You can also use the grater for quickly grating Parmesan cheese or other types of hard cheese or for grating fresh ginger or chocolate.

VEGETABLE PEELER: Use it for thinly peeling the skin off carrots, potatoes, and more. It makes great garnishes, too, so use it to make strips of chocolate, Parmesan cheese, or curls of citrus peel.

CUTTING BOARDS:

You probably will never pick up a knife without picking up a cutting board, too, so if a good knife is the most important tool in your kitchen, a cutting board ranks toward the top. Gone are the days of your mom's or grandma's kitchen when one old wooden cutting board leaned against the backsplash. Today there are choices in materials, colors, and sizes and each offers benefits.

A good cutting board should feel secure and not slip around the counter as you use it. While you might think that a super-slick surface would be ideal, the opposite is true. Ideally, it should have just a little texture so that the knife does not inadvertently slip across the surface while you are chopping, nor should the surface be so hard that the knife wears or dulls as you slice.

MATERIALS:

Many materials fit the bill and will make a great choice.

Wooden boards are classic and generally they are the easiest on the knife blade. Those made of bamboo are often more expensive but may last longer than other hardwoods. Wooden boards require a little more care than plastic boards, as they are not dishwasher safe, and to extend their life, you should oil the surface occasionally with mineral oil.

Plastic boards are colorful and dishwasher safe. They are often the least expensive.

Tempered glass, marble, or ceramic boards are available and many are beautiful. They are heavy, but are very durable and sanitary and often are heatproof so it is a great surface on which to set a hot pan. The sound of knives clipping against the hard surface may be irritating to some and the hard surface is harder on the knife blade.

CARE AND CLEANING:

Take care to avoid cross-contamination and, ideally, use two different boards. Use one for raw meat, poultry, and seafood and another board for bread and produce. It is great to color-code the boards to make it easy to identify them, or choose a different size, shape, or look for each separate task.

Cleanliness is very important for all boards. Wash them in hot, soapy water after each use, or if dishwasher safe, wash them in the dishwasher. To sanitize a cutting board, mix 1 tablespoon of unscented liquid chlorine bleach in 1 gallon of water, flood the surface of the board, covering it completely. Rinse well and dry.

No matter the material, replace boards that become scratched or deeply marred, as the grooves can harbor bacteria.

UTENSILS:

Round out your kitchen with basic utensils. Among the basics are the following:

CAN OPENER: Every kitchen needs a can opener. Whether you choose an electric or a manual one is a matter of personal choice and may be dependent upon how often you use canned food versus fresh.

CITRUS JUICER: The juice from a freshly squeezed lemon, lime, or orange will add a much better flavor to the dish or salad dressing you are preparing. With a handy citrus juicer, it takes just a minute to juice the fruit and you will not be tempted to use a bottled juice. There is no need to have a large electric juicer when an inexpensive smaller juicer or handheld reamer will quickly handle the job.

COLANDER: You will find you frequently reach for a colander to drain pasta or potatoes, or the fat from ground meat.

COOKING SPOON: The classic was made of wood, and that still is a great choice. Newer ones are made of such materials as stainless steel and heatproof plastic, which offer bright colors and fun designs. If you will be using nonstick cookware be sure to use a plastic or wooden spoon to avoid marring the nonstick finish.

CORKSCREW AND BOTTLE OPENER: Yes, they are bar tools, but you may find you reach for them often when cooking, since wine, beer, and spirits are common recipe ingredients.

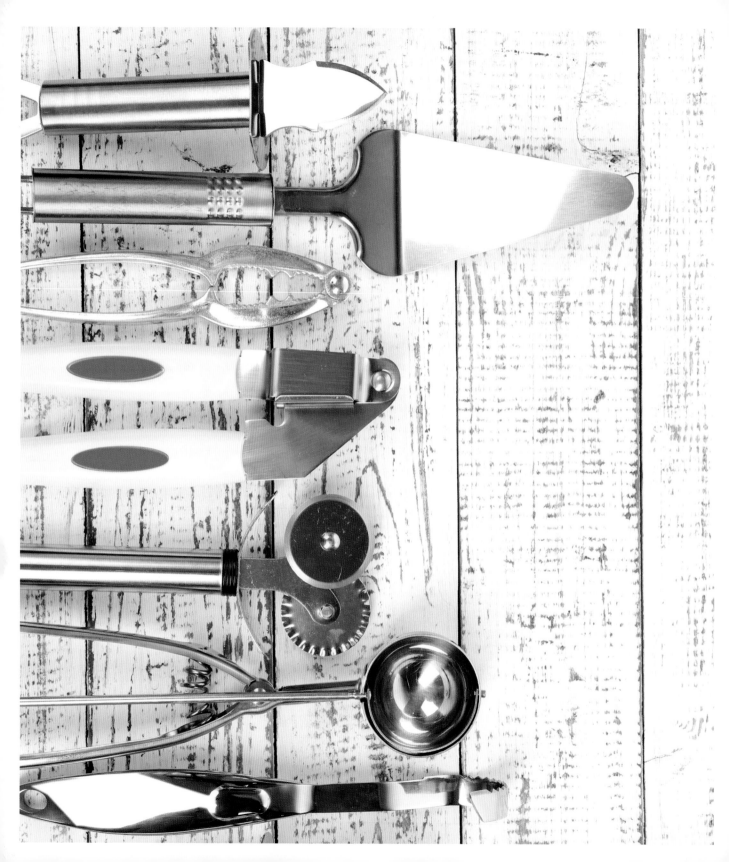

PANCAKE TURNER: While chefs or food professionals may not agree with this name, it is popular in some regions of the country to call it a spatula. No matter what you call it, you might choose both a flexible metal and a nylon or heatproof plastic for use in different pans. While nonstick finishes are harder and more resistant to scratches today, some manufacturers still recommend that you avoid using metal utensils in nonstick pans. We always choose a very thin and flexible turner to use when baking cookies as we want to lift the edge of the hot cookies without breaking them. A large, firm or stiff turner is ideal for lifting heavier meats, sandwiches, pizza, or vegetables.

PASTRY BRUSH: Use a brush to spread melted butter over dough, olive oil over slices of French bread, or sauce over grilled meat. Silicone bristles stay flexible after repeated washings and are easier to keep clean.

ROLLING PIN: There are so many new designs to choose from, but a trusty rolling pin is needed to roll out dough for pastry crusts or cookies.

SLOTTED SPOON: A must in every kitchen, a slotted spoon makes it easy to spoon out vegetables, cooked bacon, or other foods from their cooking liquid or fat.

SPATULA: This is sometimes referred to as a rubber scraper. Be sure it is heatproof, and if not, do not use it in hot foods or while cooking.

STRAINER: A fine-mesh strainer, or even two or three different sizes of strainers are used often for small tasks like draining a can of artichokes or for larger jobs like straining the cooked meat and bones from a stock.

TONGS: Avoid piercing meat with a fork when you turn it; piercing can cause juices to drain away. Instead, choose tongs for that job.

WHISK: You may want a variety of sizes, selecting a larger one for whisking several eggs at once and a smaller one for whisking a small amount of salad dressing. A whisk is the tool of choice for combining dry ingredients prior to making cookies or a cake. You are doing so much more than just combining the ingredients—whisking is essential to aerating the flour. When cooking, you will find a whisk is perfect for making a lump-free sauce.

VEGETABLE BRUSH: While it once may have been viewed as unnecessary, current food safety guidelines emphasize washing produce, especially cantaloupe and others with tough outer skin, with a stiff brush.

SPECIALTY UTENSILS:

PASTRY CUTTER OR BLENDER: This handle with parallel sturdy blades or wires is used to cut cold butter or vegetable shortening into flour for pastry.

MEAT TENDERIZER: While we may not frequently tenderize meat anymore, we often pound meat to make it thinner. Purchase one with a smooth side so you can use it to pound chicken or pork cutlets into a thin cut that will cook quickly and evenly. If you don't have one, a heavy pan, can, or rolling pin will suffice.

SCOOPS: Yes, a sturdy ice cream scoop is more than a luxury. Dipping out solid ice cream can be a chore without a heavy-duty scoop. You will also find that spring-loaded scoops, available in a variety of sizes, are convenient to use when scooping meatballs, cookie dough, or melon balls.

MEAT THERMOMETER:

We always recommend using a meat thermometer. It is great to check if meat is cooked to a safe temperature, but even more, it is an ideal way to accurately gauge doneness and ensure that every piece of meat you cook is cooked to perfection! No more over- or undercooking a piece of meat.

Today's meat cuts are different from those your mom may have purchased a few years ago. The meat may be leaner or the animal may have been allowed to feed on only grass or grains and overcooking may result in a dry cut of meat.

Some thermometers are oven safe, so you can leave the thermometer in the meat as it cooks. Others are instant-read thermometers and are not heatproof so you take the meat out of the oven and quickly check the temperature, then return the meat to the oven.

Insert the thermometer into the meaty center of the meat, away from fat and bone.

What are "rest times" and why should you bother?

Meat is quite hot when you take it out of the oven or off the grill and that residual heat continues to cook the meat, increasing the internal temperatures. All meat will taste more juicy and flavorful if you allow it to rest for 5 to 10 minutes before cutting and serving. If you want to serve a piece of meat that is still a bit pink, like a good steak, chop, or roast, you can take the meat out of the oven at the minimum temperature, cover, and allow it to rest for at least 5 minutes.

What temperature is the minimum for food safety?

With new research and food standards, the minimum safe temperatures are occasionally updated by the U.S. Department of Agriculture (USDA). To stay up-to-date, visit their website at www.usda.gov and follow the links to food safety. Remember, the color of the meat (inside or out) is not a good or reliable indicator of doneness. Follow these guidelines:

» GROUND BEEF:	160°F
» BEEF STEAKS AND ROASTS:	145°F, then rest for 5 minutes for medium-rare doneness
	155°F, then rest for 5 minutes for medium doneness
» CHICKEN & TURKEY, WHOLE, PIECES, OR GROUND:	165°F
» CASSEROLES AND LEFTOVERS:	165°F
» EGG DISHES:	160°F
» FISH:	145°F, or until fish is opaque and flakes with a fork
» PORK ROASTS AND CHOPS:	145°F, then rest for 5 minutes

203

MEASURING EQUIPMENT:

DRY: These are the nesting cups that generally come in 1, ½, ⅓, and ¼ cup measures. It is important to use these when measuring flour, sugar, or other dry ingredients so you can level off the top with a flat edge, such as a table knife.

LIQUID: This clear, marked cup with a spout is the tool to use when measuring any liquid. Do not measure dry ingredients in this cup—you may be tempted to shake the cup to try to level it off and that will compact the flour and cause incorrect measurements. In addition, due to its design you cannot level off the dry ingredients, so an incorrect measurement will result.

MEASURING SPOONS: These spoons will be used constantly! Note that a teaspoon measuring spoon does not equal a typical teaspoon you use to eat with, so keep the measuring spoons handy.

TIPS FOR MEASURING:

» If measuring a sticky ingredient, like honey, molasses, syrup, peanut butter, or solid vegetable shortening, spray the cup or spoon first with nonstick spray. The sticky ingredient will come out of the measuring cup or spoon much more easily.

» If baking becomes your passion, invest in a kitchen scale for the most accurate measurements.

POTS & PANS:

While the bright and shiny pots hanging on the rack look sexy and chic, pots and pans are made to be used, and quality cookware makes it easier to get the best results.

Did you register for a set of pans . . . and unwrap the ones you wanted? If you are still searching for the best cookware, use these tips to select them.

Avoid cheap, thin, flimsy pans. Thin ones warp or dent, and food will scorch easily.

Buy pots and pans as if making a sound investment, as the set you select may last a lifetime. Study the materials and finishes and try to understand the pros and cons each material offers. Pick them up to see if they feel balanced and comfortable to lift. Check the feel of the handle in your hands. Are the handles oven safe? Will the handles stay relatively cool? Most important, do not buy a set based on looks, or a designer name, and do not select the highest-priced one thinking it is the best set. Evaluate your needs and the foods you intend to cook and make the best selection possible.

What type of range do you have now, or what is top on your list when you can purchase a range or remodel the kitchen? If you will be using an induction range, be sure the pans contain iron (sometimes called ferromagnetic materials). If you have a smooth, glass-top range, be sure the bottom of the pans is smooth and avoid retro cast-iron pans that have a rough surface or unglazed ring.

No one set of pans does everything best for everyone—and even if you select a set, you may want to supplement with specific pieces. Add a wok, grill pan, or cast-iron skillet if these cooking styles are part of your skills, or add a pasta pot or omelet pan if you often cook these foods.

MATERIALS:

ALUMINUM: Aluminum is a great conductor of heat, so it heats quickly and evenly. It is a popular choice since it is lighter in weight. However, it reacts with some foods, especially acidic foods such as tomatoes or vinegar, and it stains. To prevent the reaction, it is often covered with stainless steel or is treated so as not to react.

COPPER: The best conductor, it heats up (and cools off) quickly. It is expensive, hard to maintain, and softer, so it dents. It reacts with some foods, so sometimes copper pans are lined with stainless steel.

STAINLESS STEEL: While pretty, stainless steel is a poor conductor of heat, so it develops hot spots and cooks unevenly. A stainless-steel pan is often constructed with a heat-conducting core of aluminum or copper.

CAST IRON: Cast iron conducts heat slowly and retains the heat. It is durable so it can last a lifetime, but it may be difficult to handle as it is heavy. An unseasoned cast-iron pan reacts with acidic foods and can rust. It is porous so it should not be soaked in soapy water or run through the dishwasher. Because of the reactions and potential for rusting, cast-iron pans are often coated with porcelain enamel. A highly seasoned cast-iron pan, even one you might inherit from Grandma, develops a slick surface from the years of use. A new, uncoated cast-iron pan should be seasoned before use. To do so, line the bottom rack of the oven with aluminum foil, then preheat the oven to 350°F. Rub the pan, inside and out, with a coating of vegetable oil or melted vegetable shortening. Place the pan upside down on the top oven rack. Bake for 1 hour. Allow it to cool, and it is ready to use.

GLASS OR CERAMIC: While once glass or ceramic pans for stovetop cooking were available, they are no longer common, and instead this material is used for casserole dishes and ovenware.

FINISHES:

PORCELAIN ENAMEL: A smooth, glassy finish, often used on cast-iron, it not only adds color, it makes the pan stain and scratch resistant. Since it is slick, foods often do not stick to the surface.

ANODIZED: This finish means the surface is oxidized, so the aluminum becomes nonporous and nonreactive. Food barely sticks, and the aluminum surface is easier to clean. Since tomatoes, wine, and other acidic foods do not react with the surface, many aluminum pans are now anodized.

NONSTICK: The durability of nonstick cookware has improved, but many manufacturers still recommend using nylon, plastic, or wood utensils and warn against using abrasive cleaners on the surface. Often, manufacturers of nonstick cookware do not recommend using high heat, and if that is the case, it is not the best pan to use for searing or browning meat. While nonstick pans are safe, there are still questions about the manufacturing process and some suggestions of health concerns, so some people wish to avoid this finish. However, if you enjoy cooking eggs or making cheese sauce, you might want a nonstick skillet and pan in your arsenal.

SIZES AND SHAPES:

Below is a list of common pots and pans, and how many you might want of each.

SKILLETS: Many kitchens begin with a small (6- to 8-inch), medium (10-inch), and large (12-inch) skillet. Many skillets are sold without covers, so if you want to cover and simmer foods, you may want to add a cover; sometimes it is sold separately. If you want to oven-bake in the skillet, choose oven-safe varieties, or note the material used for the handles and evaluate if it is oven safe.

SAUCEPANS OR POTS: Select a range of sizes, from small (1-quart) to large (4-to-6 quart). The volume is measured by filling to "flooding," so the full volume of the pan may not be usable (for example, the usable capacity of a 2-quart pan is about 6 cups, or 1½ quarts).

DUTCH OVEN: This larger covered pan holds 6 to 12 quarts and is ideal for soups, stews, chilies, and other dishes that are braised or stewed. Traditionally this pot or kettle was made of cast iron, was oven safe, and was quite heavy. Many brands and sets of pots and pans now include a Dutch oven so they are available in a variety of materials and finishes.

STOCKPOT: This tall pot is ideal for soups, stocks, stews, chilies, and other large dishes. It is also the pan most suited to cooking pasta or boiling a large quantity of water. Some stockpots today come with a perforated pasta insert. Avoid stockpots that are made of a thin metal; the soup or chili will easily scorch on the bottom if not stirred very frequently.

GRILL PAN: A heavy pan, similar to a skillet, but formed with ridges across the bottom so the fat can drain away from the meat as it cooks. The shallow sides of a grill pan also make it easy to turn the meat.

GRIDDLE: Griddles are available in electric or stovetop models and are perfect for cooking foods that do not require a lot of fat or liquid. Specialties include pancakes, French toast, and grilled sandwiches.

BAKEWARE:

Do either of you like to bake? Even if you say "not really," you need a selection of bakeware—and if you love to bake, then selecting an array of quality bakeware goes without saying. Every kitchen needs pans and casseroles safe for oven baking. Even if you are not baking artisan breads, the oven will be used frequently to reheat, brown, broil, roast, braise, and bake a range of foods—from the most intricate gourmet dishes to convenient mixes.

Quality bakeware lets you become the master of the oven. Choose the right pans or dishes and you will find that foods bake better. The results will be more even, for you will be less likely to burn the bottoms of the cookies, overbrown the edges of the brownies, or serve underdone, still-cold-in-the-center main dishes.

MATERIALS:

ALUMINUM: Aluminum is always a favorite in the kitchen because it transfers heat evenly. Baking (or cookie) sheets and cake pans made of aluminum bake evenly. When new, the finish is often bright and shiny, but untreated aluminum can discolor as it reacts with certain foods, especially acidic foods such as tomatoes or vinegar.

STAINLESS STEEL: This material is known for shiny pans—a plus when baking lightly colored cakes and cookies—but it does not transfer the heat evenly.

CERAMIC, POTTERY, OR GLASS: These materials transfer heat slowly, which means they heat up slowly and cool off slowly. Square and rectangular baking dishes, pie plates, loaf

COMMON BAKEWARE:

Below is a list of common bakeware items and how many you might want to have in your kitchen.

BAKING SHEET OR COOKIE SHEET

13 x 18 inches	2

CAKE PANS

Round, 8 or 9 x 2-inch	2
Square, 8 or 9 x 2-inch	2

LOAF PANS

8 x 4 x 2½-inch or 9 x 5 x 3-inch	2

RECTANGULAR BAKERS

9 x 13 x 2-inch	1
7 x 11 x 2-inch	1

PIE PLATES

9-inch (regular and deep-dish)	1
Individual (about 4¼ inches in diameter)	2

TART PANS

About 4½-inches in diameter	2

PIZZA PAN

12 inches in diameter	1

CASSEROLE DISHES

1-, 2-, or 3-quart	1 of each size

COOLING RACKS

Available in a variety of sizes, these are indispensable, and if you bake you will need one or two cooling racks.

pans, and many casseroles are made of ceramic, pottery, or glass. These dishes are often safe for use in the microwave, too. Sudden temperature changes will cause many glass, ceramic, and pottery pieces to break, so allow them to cool before washing and do not pour cold liquids into hot casserole dishes. Read the label, as some are safe for freezer-to-oven use while others specifically recommend against using them under the broiler or on a burner of the stove. Some are safe to place in a hot, preheated oven while some specialty items, especially those handmade by a local potter, should be placed in a cold oven to allow the dish, food, and oven to heat together to avoid any possibility of cracking.

SILICONE: Flexible silicone (or what we often call "plastic") bakeware is fun due to the variety of colors and shapes available. Foods do not stick to the slick surface. They can go directly from the freezer to the oven and most are safe in the microwave. Do not place them on a hot burner. These pans can be cut or damaged with knives or scissors.

FINISHES:

Gleaming bakeware is readily available untreated, and many cooks choose shiny cookie sheets or cake pans without added finishes but you may also choose from an array of finishes. What do those finishes offer and how can you make a wise selection?

NONSTICK: If you select nonstick bakeware, double check the use information as you may need to avoid metal tools that might scratch and scouring with stiff brushes or steel wool. Evaluate the color: Darker finishes, often typical of nonstick, will absorb heat so your cookies and cakes may brown more. Today, many cooks will line baking sheets and cake pans with parchment paper, which means foods do not stick and clean up is a snap, so a nonstick finish is less important.

ANODIZED: The surface is oxidized, making it nonporous, so foods stick less. Anodizing also prevents discoloration from acidic foods, but it may make the surface dark, and delicate cakes or light-colored sugar cookies will brown more quickly or too much.

PORCELAIN COATED OR PORCELAIN ENAMEL: This smooth, glassy finish is often used on cast iron. It not only adds color, but it makes the pan stain and scratch resistant and prevents rust. Since the coating is slick, foods often do not stick to the surface. Porcelain might be found on casserole dishes, pie pans, loaf pans, and rectangular baking dishes.

OTHER FEATURES TO CONSIDER:

GAUGE: A pan's gauge is the thickness of the metal or glass. Thin metals may be less expensive to purchase, but may be trickier to use in the oven as they will develop hot spots or scorch. Thin metal is more likely to warp or dent. Choose pans, of any material, that seem heavy for their size.

SIZE: Commercial, recognized manufacturers generally adhere to fairly standard sizes for most bakeware, but read the label as there are still variations. Bakeware sizes are listed by the dimensions (which are taken at the top inside edge) or by the volume capacity (which, as with saucepans, equals the capacity filled to overflowing, so the usable capacity for a 3-quart baking dish will be about 2½ quarts). Specialty manufacturers may offer unique sizes and shapes, which are fun when selecting a mold or cake pan, but may be challenging when you need to know if your casserole or favorite cake recipe will fit.

SHINY OR DARK: A shiny surface reflects heat, which minimizes overbrowning and is good when baking cookies, biscuits, or a layer cake. A dark finish on the surface absorbs heat so cookies or biscuits baked on a dark baking sheet often brown quickly, so the bottoms of the cookies may become overly brown before they are baked through.

TIPS FOR BAKEWARE:

Glass or ceramic dishes retain heat, so you can reduce the oven temperature by 25°F.

The size, weight, and material of the bakeware may affect the baking time, especially for cakes, cookies, and brownies or other items that are baked for shorter baking times. Check the baked good at the minimum baking time listed in the recipe, then continue baking as needed.

If you are thinking about greasing or buttering a pan, be sure to check your recipe because some cookies spread out too much when placed on a greased sheet. Cakes, except angel food cakes, and breads are generally baked in a greased or buttered pan (and many recipes now recommend lining the pan with parchment paper as well).

ACKNOWLEDGMENTS

Recipes and photos become a finished, cherished cookbook only with the support and hard work of many people, and we are grateful for each of you!

We appreciate the love and support of our families. We have each been married for many years, so we see our days as "newlyweds" only in a rearview mirror. Marriage is not always easy, but we have been blessed by many years of love and support. We each have wonderful families who encourage us. Our hope is that each newlywed who reads and cooks from this book is able to share in a wonderful, loving relationship for many years to come.

Roxanne's husband, Bob Bateman, and her daughter, Grace, are the loves of her life and the lights of her life. Thank you for each and every day, and for tasting, testing, and supporting her down to the last bite, crumb, and dirty dish. Also, a special thank-you to Roxanne's parents, who have been married for sixty-four years and are her biggest heroes. They provide the template for what marriage is all about.

Kathy's family, David, Laura, and Amanda, are the center of her world. She cherishes their constant love and support. Their smiles, laughter, and friendship make each day special.

We want to thank our agents, Lisa Ekus and Sally Ekus, and the entire staff at The Lisa Ekus Group, LLC, for expert insight and advice, coupled with patience and friendship! Thank you.

Thank you to BJ Berti, Courtney Littler, Michelle McMillian, and everyone at St. Martin's Press for creating such a wonderful book and for their professionalism beyond compare. Thank you!

We appreciate the creative and dedicated talent of photographer David Shaughnessy. He became our teammate in this book, and we are grateful for his skill and hard work. Thanks to Andrea Krakow for lending a hand on the food styling.

We are blessed by many incredible people who support us and our work! Please know we appreciate each of you. Most of all, we are blessed to work together as friends. Our thirty-year career path has been side by side, in test kitchens, as consultants, and as authors. We cherish our friendship and that makes the journey so much more fun and rewarding.

With Appreciation to:

Louise Myers, Pryde's Kitchen and Home, "The Hardware Store For Cooks," Kansas City, MO. www.prydeskitchen.com. Thank you, Louise, for the beautiful dishes, appliances, and utensils that added so much to the photos and for allowing us access to this extraordinary shop for beautiful photos.

The Fresh Market, Overland Park, KS. Manager, Bolar Brown. www.thefreshmarket.com. Thank you for allowing us access to the store for location photos.

Thanks to Brian Heydon for graciously allowing photographs in his beautiful home.

Thank you to each of the following individuals who shared their time posing for photographs: Craig and Claudia Donnell, Erin and Kevin Whaley, Joshua and Nellie Sparkman, Kaitlin Byrne, Joe Privitera, Jessica Roland, Jeff Schloack, Chelsea and Nate Templeton, Brady Jansen, Carrington Reyes, Suzanne Kerr, and Ryan Motter. You were all wonderful.

INDEX